THIS IS RESCUE

THE STORY OF OUR LITTLE RED BARN

MOLLY TOTORO

CONTENTS

INTRODUCTION

I FIRST LEARNED of Always and Furever from a Facebook post. A casual acquaintance shared a photo of a cute little dog, and I followed the link. We recently lost our beloved Bassett, and I desperately missed his presence in my life.

Like most followers of The Barn, I stalked their page. I scrolled through photos first thing in the morning, and I went to bed watching Jason's good night videos.

Six weeks later I attended the required volunteer training. At least thirty of us, all ages and sizes, found a pup to snuggle on a blanketed couch as we listened to Stephanie explain the ins-and-outs of rescue. The next Monday morning I was at The Barn, happily folding laundry, picking up poop, and loving on the dogs. I knew I found my paradise on earth.

Two weeks later we fostered our first dog, Dusty, an old gentle lab-mix who came from a home filled with 73 cats! I promoted Dusty on social media. I took him to adoption events. But as the saying goes... the dog chooses us. Three weeks later we foster-failed, and Dusty (now Buddy) became a part of our family. This, I've learned, is a well-known hazard of foster care.

A month later we fostered Hero (see his story on page 143). If we only had the space, I would gladly adopt every Labrador that comes into The Barn. So I looked for another way to help save these precious furry souls.

This book is intended to share Jen's dream. It tells her story as well as some of the stories of dedicated staff and volunteers. But primarily, this book focuses on the dogs — their heartbreaking stories that transform into happily ever afters.

To that end, every photo in the book is an A&F dog. Their soulful eyes and smiling faces showcase their individual personalities.

ALL profits from the sale of this book will go to A&F — to help them rescue and care for the dogs that need a furever home.

If you'd like to learn more about The Barn, please visit their website: https://alwaysandfurever.love

~ Molly Totoro

PART ONE
HUMBLE BEGINNINGS

Dogs do speak, but only to
those who know how to listen.

~ Orhan Pamuk

JEN'S STORY

WHEN JEN DULSKI was a young girl she had two dreams: to become an Olympic figure skater and to save dogs.

Her skating dreams came to an end when she was thirteen years old. The death of her maternal grandparents had a profound impact on the family. Not long after, her father lost his job. Jen's immediate reaction was: how can I help? This was a common theme throughout her life.

At fourteen, Jen took a job at the local Jack-in-the-Box to contribute to the family income and reduce some financial stress. This desire to help her family so they would no longer worry about money influenced her decision to become a lawyer.

Jen's law career took her to Pennsylvania, back to Illinois, and then to Boston, MA. It was there Jen's life changed dramatically. In June 2015, her best friend died suddenly from a drug overdose. "The pain of losing one's soulmate is crushing, and grief has a way of sucking life out of the living."

For the next eighteen months Jen survived by going to work, crying, and praying, "God, please let me get through this."

In January 2017 Jen made a radical move from Boston to Overland Park, Kansas. She took a drastic pay cut to live in the middle of nowhere, but she knew she needed a change.

A few weeks later, Jen had a crazy, wonderful, impossible idea. "I'm going to buy a farm and start a dog rescue."

The idea made no sense. And it was absolutely perfect.

Jen and her beloved Penny

THE BARN

It started outside a General Nutrition Center. In 2017, Jen Dulski moved from Boston to Kansas City. She knew nothing about the area, but she knew she needed a change. As she stood outside the retailer's doors, an idea from the past flooded her memory: Buy a farm and open a dog sanctuary.

While Jen owned two senior dogs, she had no background in dog rescue. She was a city girl. All things bug and nature-related terrified her. The idea made no sense except... it reawakened her young girl's dream of saving dogs.

God opened the door, and Jen walked through. "God put the right people in my life at the right time and continues to do so every day. Together my one dream has become the dream and reality for so many."

Through an online grief support group, Jen met a woman who introduced her to a local realtor.

That local realtor knew a family who might be ready to sell their farm.

Jen and the family connected over shared grief experiences. They sold her The Barn for the exact amount she could afford.

"The family that sold me this farm named it the Ever After Farm. In her wonderful note to me the first day I moved in, she reminded me it will be hard work but to always remember it's never too late for happily ever after. And that is where our motto began."

Things were coming together, but not without a lot of faith, hope, and endurance. Jen had to apply five times for a building loan before someone saw the potential.

That $100,000 loan lasted about three months. She applied for another. And another. And when she could no longer qualify for a loan, she maxed out her credit cards. That's the power of a dream. You do what it takes.

"When the credit cards were maxed I mostly cried, worried beyond belief and prayed. And at the end of the year I received a promotion at work."

Walking by faith. Doing the work.

Jen committed to paying off the loans herself. All funds raised through donations go directly to the dogs. There is no adoption fee because "we just don't believe in buying a life. Dogs aren't property and you cannot put a price on saving a soul."

In a year's time, The Barn opened its doors on May 12, 2018.

While the focus is saving the lives of senior dogs... those who are neglected, forgotten, and left to die... The Barn also saves us. "This little red Barn isn't just the pups' sanctuary. It's the sanctuary of an entire little city in Kansas as well as the Facebook community that follows us. All these dogs saved me. And while our hearts are broken when they leave us, it is worth it. Because every new pup we save allows us to fill their hearts with peace before they leave this earth."

Faith and Love built this Barn. Faith and Love will keep it going. "Everyone has a story. The Barn is full of second chances — for all the pups and volunteers. A second chance to know love and find a bit of peace, even if for a moment."

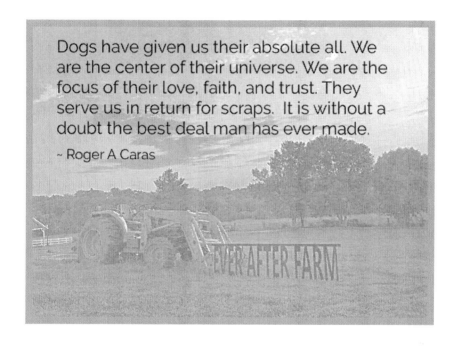

Dogs have given us their absolute all. We are the center of their universe. We are the focus of their love, faith, and trust. They serve us in return for scraps. It is without a doubt the best deal man has ever made.

~ Roger A Caras

DAISY

Miss Daisy was Always & Furever's first rescue. In October 2017, long before Ever After Farm's Barn was open, we received a message that a dog was left alone — living outside in horrible thunderstorms. Jen and her neighbor, Stephanie, showed up without a crate or a leash and told one another to pretend they knew what they were doing.

When we first met her, Daisy was chained to an outdoor kennel. She had spent nearly all her life outdoors. Miss Daisy stole our hearts from the moment we saw her big beautiful sad eyes peering at us under the fence.

The good folks at Kerry's Kennel in Spring Hill were kind enough to keep her the first night until the veterinarian could see her the following day. Despite her life of isolation, Miss Daisy was a sweet lady — a little shy at first but eager and happy to make friends.

The next day at Spring Hill Veterinary Clinic we learned that Miss Daisy had a mammary gland mass that needed to be removed. A quickly organized GoFundMe campaign successfully raised money to pay for the surgery. Meanwhile, since the sanctuary was still under construction, Jen arranged for a friend to foster her.

Miss Daisy's treatment went well, and the news was good: the mass was benign. Scott, her new foster dad, arrived at the clinic as soon as the vet cleared her to leave. Scott and Miss Daisy bonded immediately.

By the time they arrived at Scott's house, he and Miss Daisy decided they were meant to be. Scott called Jen and asked if he could permanently adopt Miss Daisy. At that point, she became simply Daisy and quickly settled in at her new forever home with her new forever dad.

Daisy is the first dog to exemplify our belief that every senior dog deserves a happily ever after.

I have found that when you are deeply troubled, there are things you get from the silent devoted companionship of a dog that you can get from no other source.
- Doris Day

THE ORIGINAL SIX

ANNIE:

Annie was the first dog to come into our care — on the day we opened! We couldn't tell by her happy-go-lucky personality this sweet girl had lived most of her life confined by a chain. Fortunately for her (and for us) a good Samaritan convinced her owner to relinquish her to Always and Furever.

Annie was usually the first smiling face that met anyone who came to The Barn. And while her age showed in the gray on her muzzle and the reoccurring tumor on her neck, she was full of enough puppy energy to play a few rounds of fetch or sneak any food she could steal from volunteers and other residents.

Annie waited for just the right family to walk through the door. But once they arrived, she was ready to leave the nest. She jumped into the arms of her future momma and kissed her way into their hearts. She chose them, and they unequivocally gave Annie the best year and a half of her life.

Annie crossed Rainbow Bridge on February 13, 2020, but she will forever remain in our hearts.

MILES:

Miles came to The Barn the day after Annie.

Miles was found as a stray, wondering the streets on a bitter cold February evening. The local vet took him in for the night but had no room to keep him. They had no choice but to schedule his euthanation for the next day.

Jen worked with a local kennel who agreed to keep Miles for the next three months until The Barn was complete.

While we knew little about Miles' past, his kind, sweet, and gentle disposition was clear. Miles wasn't the guy at the front of the pack looking for attention. Instead, he was content to wait patiently at the back of the pack for any leftover love directed his way. This sweet old man didn't keep his distance out of fear. He just wasn't a pushy guy.

His soft fluffy coat made him easy to love on, but his gentle laid-back ways often made him easy to overlook. However, word-of-mouth is our best resource. A faithful volunteer shared his story with her aunt, who eventually adopted Miles and spoiled him the rest of his days. Miles passed on August 10, 2019, surrounded by his loving family.

HANK:

A few days later, Hank arrived at The Barn. Those who knew Hank described him as GIANT, gentle, protective, sweet, caring, and as playful as his aging body would allow. When anyone arrived at Always and Furever, Hank greeted them by sticking his giant head out the doggie door. With his deep bark, he said, somewhat impatiently, to come love on him.

The family who owned this eight-year-old Great Dane sadly surrendered him to A&F because they could no longer care for him in their home. Too many stairs for his old legs. But Jen had connections.

Her good friend Lorraine had already planned to visit The Barn. Jen wagered a bet that she would leave with a dog, even though Lorraine freely confessed she was not a dog-person. All it took was one look at Hank and she was smitten: *I followed him around the WHOLE weekend, trying to make him love me too. Lol. All I wanted to do was smuggle him home (to Pittsburgh) in my suitcase. All 145 pounds of him.*

But The Barn is where dreams come true — for dogs and people. A long-distance Freedom Drive took Hank from Kansas to his furever home in Pittsburgh.

Hank even became a celebrity of sorts. He had his own FaceBook page, *Hank's Haven*, with over ten thousand followers and one video garnering "viral" status with nearly ten million views. Hank lived his best life in Pittsburgh until he crossed Rainbow Bridge on June 22, 2019. Hank may be gone, but he will never be forgotten.

BERNADETTE:

Less than a month later The Barn went from three dogs to six: *When we went to grab Bernadette, we couldn't leave Penny behind, so she was unexpected. And we couldn't turn Howard away since his number was up.*

Love and compassion for the lost and forgotten is what The Barn is all about.

Bernie was our first blind resident. She was a fiery gal who often "shark bit" her fellow roommates. She taught herself the dog door after being forced to come inside wrapped in a sheet. She was resilient, bossy, and the bestest barn buddy ever. She loved going on car rides, Sonic trips, and getting belly rubs.

While Bernie arrived at The Barn blind with a body full of tumors, ticks and patchy skin, we vowed to do whatever she needed. Bernie lived another eight months at The Barn knowing all who came in contact with her loved her unconditionally.

HOWARD:

This sweet perfect boy was abandoned at a kill shelter. But fate brought him to The Barn.

Howard (Howie) came to us in June, just a day from being put down. When we say perfect, we mean it. He was sweet to all humans, dogs, cats & even squirrels. He was housebroken and could easily be left alone without fear of destruction. His favorite pastimes included car rides, playing, and sleeping throughout the day. His one vice, however, was bacon-flavored bubbles. This boy connected with his inner puppy anytime the bubbles appeared. Unfortunately, his senior joints ached afterward.

Howie welcomed one and all with a tail wag and a smile. He was a perfect companion.

While Howie never found an adopted family, he found his way into a furever foster home where they accepted and loved him as one of their own.

Sweet Howie made his way across Rainbow Bridge on April 29, 2020. We are confident the original Fab Five welcomed him with open paws and they are frolicking together in paradise.

All his life he tried to be a good person.
Many times, however, he failed. For after
all, he was only human. He wasn't a dog.

~ Charles M Schulz

PENNY LANE PUPS

PENNY:

In Jen's words:

You were our first unexpected addition and our most special. You were always under my feet, tripping me, or in my arms. You were practically perfect in every way and one of my littlest best friends. You were beautiful when we got you, when we lost you, and even more so now.

I know nothing about your past, how or why such a loving soul ended up at a kill shelter, but thank you for finding us and loving us and being a part of our family. You are more than loved. Whatever is more than love, that's what you are — not just to me, but to everyone. I wish you all the love and peace and happiness your little heart can hold in heaven, Penny.

In December 2018, there was an accident in The Barn. Someone inadvertently left a bit of food on the counter. Another dog with food aggression issues caught Penny in the wrong place at the wrong time. Even heroic vet visits could not save her.

But in the face of personal loss and grief, Jen also penned these words:

Once we take a dog into The Barn, they are a part of our family — forever, with whatever conditions, ailments or issues or baggage they carry. Whether they live with us a short time or find a new family to share their love, we love them forever. We have been aware of this dog's food aggression (and took appropriate precautions).... Remember, there is no one to blame. None of our dogs will ever be perfect but they love us perfectly and that is why for this dog and even for Penny we at least have to try.... There are only two options here. Find a no-dog home for a wonderful girl with a broken past or realize that some happy endings only begin in heaven.

Unconditional love is what The Barn is all about.

To honor her sweetheart, Jen named the driveway leading to the Little Red Barn — Penny Lane.

We use two unique hashtags to mark our social media posts: #littleredbarn

#pennylanepups

GUMP AND MAMA

Gump and Mama served as unofficial mascots for A&F. While no one plays favorites at The Barn, Gump and Mama were definitely the most popular.

They arrived at The Barn in early July 2018. The fifteenth and sixteenth residents. Another local Kansas City rescue found them chained outside a home, most likely for their entire lives. Gump was about seven years old and Opal eleven. She was a devoted Mama and could always be found near Gump's side.

Not surprisingly, both dogs were malnourished and their ears badly eaten by flies. In addition, Mama had several large tumors, and one of Gump's front legs had significant nerve damage — possibly from his attempt to escape the chains.

The Barn accepted both dogs with loving arms and tried to nurse them back to health. After exhausting all other options, however, including custom shoulder pads, meds, hormones, inner tubes, cones, and t-shirts, we decided the most humane decision for Gump's leg was amputation. This would give him a chance at a pain-free life.

In February 2019, Gump had the operation, and he quickly acclimated to the life of a tripod.

Gump ruled The Barn. If the wet food supply ran low, Gump would take to social media. Cases of wet food magically appeared at The Barn's front door. The same miracle occurred when Gump needed more string cheese. The entire A&F online community adored these two pups.

Volunteers would often take them out for daytime walks at a local park, then Sonic cheeseburger treats and pup cones. Gump quickly learned the leash meant a few hours of freedom.

With so much love and publicity, we couldn't understand why no one had yet to adopt these two. Month after month went by. But they never gave up hope.

Then in mid-December 2019, they received their Christmas miracle. Gump and Mama found their furever home. Several volunteers came to The Barn for the goodbye celebration. Everyone cried. Tears of joy tinged with sadness. Gump and Mama had become family. We would miss them greatly.

UPDATE: Gump and Mama enjoyed a glorious two months with their furever family. They knew nothing but love, comfort, and good food. Sadly, however, Mama passed in late February. It was as though she lived long enough to ensure her sweet boy found a home. Once she knew he was in good hands, she could leave and rest in peace.

If interested in following Gump's adventures, he now has his own FaceBook page: Gump Gazette (www.facebook.com/gump.havner)

Dogs are the most amazing creatures;
they give unconditional love.
For me, they are the role model
for being alive.   - Gilda Radner

IN JUST TWO YEARS...

THE BARN'S growth is exponential and the number of rescues continues to increase each month.

The list below summarizes the 2019 numbers — our first full year of operation:

- 506 dogs saved
- 32 cats saved
- 426 adoptions
- Over 90 dogs in our care on average each month: 60+ in foster homes, 20 with furever fosters
- Over $200,000 in vet bills - paid in full
- In December alone over $38,000 in vet bills paid off
- Said farewell to 65 furry friends
- Saved dogs from as far away as Louisiana, Oklahoma, Alabama, Georgia, Nebraska and Iowa. Location doesn't matter but saving lives does
- Placed dogs into homes as far away as California, Virginia,

Pennsylvania, Iowa, Nebraska, Colorado, Texas, and Illinois because (again) location doesn't matter but love does.

This is the power of a dream coupled with faith, love, dedication, and hard work.

This is rescue.

TOUCHING TESTIMONIES

SECOND YEAR ANNIVERSARY

The Barn planned to host a second year anniversary celebration on May 12, 2020. However, with Covid-19 restrictions, the large gathering was canceled. So The Barn did what it does best and took to social media.

Throughout the day, fans posted heartfelt testimonials, thanking A&F staff and volunteers for the sacrifices they make each and every day.

Here are just a few of those letters:

(*From Makayla*)

Happy, happy two-year anniversary to heaven on earth! When I say this place is magical, I truly mean it.

My family and I have been here almost since the beginning. I love being a part of A&F. Despite the sad days, the heartache, and the pain, it is worth the effort. I am blessed to witness the transformation of furry friends because they finally know and understand love.

The dogs' visible transformation accompanies an internal magic within us. These dogs teach us about unconditional love, forgiveness, unbreakable trust, and faith. These dogs (and now cats) are so generous.

My "why" is the animals. No matter how difficult their past or how mentally or physically broken they are, they still love. They still give you kisses and wag their tails. They get up and persevere through the hurt. And that is all any of us can ask.

∾

(From Tricia)

Words cannot express what The Little Red Barn means to me and my family. It is truly a healing place.

I believe like the dogs, we all have a story, and I have the opportunity to be a voice for the voiceless. The things we see and hear at times can bring us to our knees. That is where we pray and get back up and do it again each day. It is not easy and it challenges me every day.

I work with a team of people who share my same passion. A group of people who don't want to be recognized, but they are some of the best people I know. They are humble. They stay up day and night, struggling to know if they made the right decision for the dogs.

We often see the worst in people and how they treat dogs. But fortunately we have each other to see there is still good!

The dogs could not have a better group fighting for them!

This IS rescue!

Happy Trails and Fairy Tails.

∾

(From Loraine)

If I'm being totally honest, I never thought I'd own a dog. But guess what? I fell completely in love with the gentle giant Hank, and I'm about to rescue my second. It's amazing to realize almost one thousand lives were saved in between! While I still wouldn't consider myself a "dog person," I'm definitely a "Hank person."

What Jen and her team have done is nothing short of amazing. The time, patience, energy, sweat, and tears they put into this barn and these animals is beyond words.

I have since persuaded my sister and my next-door neighbor to adopt dogs from A&F.

So on this second anniversary of Always & Furever, I want to say thank you to all of You! You are inspirational and amazing.

$\sim$

(From Jane)

Almost two years ago, I moved back to the area and was looking to get involved. It didn't take long to discover my passion was these dogs and this Barn.

I started as a volunteer and had the privilege of hanging out with the original Fab Five. I soon became medical coordinator, and with the help of my 90-year-old father, went on many vet runs. I now focus on record-keeping and finances. I have had the joy of watching our rescue numbers explode.

I initially started volunteering for the dogs. But over the years, I've made many friends whom I never would have otherwise. I am honored to be a part of this team. Happy two-year anniversary A&F!

$\sim$

(From Miranda)

My daughter Julianna and I were the original night time feeders/tuck-in crew (before Jason and his master goodnight-video skills joined the team). I have always had a passion for dogs and dreamed of working with them someday. I was thrilled when I learned The Barn was right down the street from my house.

Although I no longer help with feeding, I volunteer every chance I get. I am blessed to be a part of this incredible team of people. It's truly my little slice of heaven on earth.

(From Nicki)

Do you know that feeling when you're not sad, but you just feel empty? Like something is missing? Fortunately, life led me to the place I needed to be when I needed it most.

A&F was this opportunity, and I knew it the minute my son and I walked into orientation.

While I have experienced much in just a few months, it's been a blessing to watch my kids become involved with A&F.

A&F is far more than "just" a rescue. It's about giving & getting even more love in return. It's learning to trust again. It's being surrounded by many large-hearted humans who were once strangers but are now friends. It's about bad days, sad days, and frustrating days, but all are outweighed by many more happy days. It's about the excitement of reading daily social media posts from amazing fosters & furever homes. It's the sad yet beautiful experience of holding a dog as they cross over the rainbow bridge. It's getting before-and-after pictures of dogs who visited a groomer for the first time. It's everything and more than I could have imagined. The Little Red Barn is the best kind of Rescue!

Thank you, Jen Dulski, for bringing your dream to life. And for allowing my family to be a part of it.

~

(*From Sue*)

I've been with A&F since its infancy. Jen gave me the title of Vice President, but that just means I do whatever I am told.

I was never a dog person until Jen sent me a message saying, "Hey, I want to start a Senior Sanctuary. What do you think? Want to help?" From that moment I was all in.

My second trip to The Barn I fell in love with Stuart. After I returned to Pennsylvania, I couldn't stop thinking about him. I knew this blind guy needed a furever home.

Thank you all for your love and support of Jen, the pups, and the very special little red Barn on the hill.

~

(*From Konni*)

Yahoo — it's your two-year anniversary!

What an incredible journey already. So much love, dedication and work by so many amazing people. I can't imagine all that lies ahead.

I was fortunate to discover A&F and its mission. It stands for something lived and demonstrated by so many passionate, big-hearted people. I've loved, cried, and been mad at what pups have endured by humans. But the transformations I've witnessed by pups feeling loved, safe, and fed is proof that A&F is like no other rescue. I'm such a small part, but I support it in any way I can.

∼

(*From Stephanie*)

Happy two-year anniversary A&F! It seems like a lifetime ago. I simply cannot fathom how many dogs Jen and her warriors have saved. I have many fond memories of very special dogs and all the wonderful friendships made in this special little dog community.

I met Jen in her dream stage. She was standing in the pasture that is now the circle drive and singing with earphones in. Mugs and Lib were at her side.

In Jen's authentic style, the old barn quickly became the Little Red Barn.

We went on our first rescue to retrieve Daisy. We tried to act like we knew what we were doing, but we learned our first lesson of dog rescue: take a leash!

In the early days, I took Lucy for the day — a skinny and scabby A&F pup. I forgot to tell Jen I was taking her and also forgot to tell her I was adopting her. Jen figured it out when she saw me coming to The Barn with Lucy in tow, wearing one of my scarves.

So many wonderful memories and friends. I look forward to many more. Congratulations Jen and your dream team...you are all a force to be reckoned with.

∼

(*From Kelly*)

Two years ago a good friend sent me an email about a senior dog sanctuary opening in Spring Hill, KS. Little did I know how much this place would change my life.

These dogs give me unconditional love, even when I'm not deserving. These furry souls kiss the tears from my face when I'm hurting. They bring me joy as I see their smiling faces on a car ride.

They don't care about the color of my skin, whether I'm a boy or a girl, whether I like boys or girls, or whether I'm a size 0 or 24. They just love. Something our world needs to be better at — especially now.

So thank you, Jen, for following your dreams and for allowing me to be a small part of this little red Barn. It's made me a better person. Happy two years A&F!

~

(*From Megan*)

Happy second anniversary!

I walked into Always and Furever for orientation four months after they opened. I felt nothing but love from the moment I walked through the door. Love from the animals, love from the volunteers signing people in, and love and passion from Jen talking about The Barn and her plans. She explained volunteers could walk dogs, pick up poo, or just love on the dogs because that is what they crave when we come to The Barn.

The first time I came to volunteer happened to be workout night. Since I was wearing jeans, an attire not suited for jumping jacks, I took a dog for a walk. However, big ole lovable Hank wouldn't make room for me to get out of the gate. I asked for help. But Jen assured me (between yelling workout orders) that Hank was chill and would stay by me.

So we went out the gate, and Hank proceeded to run away. I couldn't believe I was going to lose a dog my first night. Fortunately, the dog I was walking could outrun the loping Hank. We managed to put a collar on Hank and steer him back to The Barn.

I became more involved and began helping with events. I've gained some of the best friendships and can't imagine my life without them or the dogs of the Little Red Barn.

Here's to Year Two and many more!

~

(*From Joanne*)

Happy second anniversary to A&F!

We are thankful to be a small part of the bigger picture. I found the Little Red Barn when it first opened and had one or two dogs. My daughter fell in love with Annie and Hank. Then she fell in love with Miles, Penny, Bernie, Scooby, and the list goes on. The Barn is a good place to learn, grow, love, and accept. It is especially good for kids to see a successful community-minded mission and people helping because they care. Thank you, Little Red Barn for all you do. We look forward to the years ahead. Lots of love to you all.

~

(*From Amanda*)

It's hard to put into words what Always and Furever means to me and the difference it's made in my life.

I lost my senior dog in 2018. He was my "heart dog," as they say, and it was excruciating.

I started watching the Little Red Barn's videos and fell in love with their mission. I thought it would be a "fun" place to volunteer and I could get my dog fix. However, it soon became so much more.

Initially, my volunteer work involved sitting on the couch and petting the dogs. I did this for a few months until I saw a post about a sad little boxer with a dislocated hip. I impulsively offered to foster for two weeks. At the end of that time, I signed the contract, and she became mine forever. The best decision I've ever made.

Recently my traveling schedule decreased, and I fostered again. First Macon and Marley and then Dusty. I was home with Dusty for only an hour when she jumped my fence! Immediately alerted A&F and within half an hour over 20 volunteers arrived in my neighborhood to help me search, hang up flyers, call shelters and simply check on me.

I apologized profusely to Jen, and the support I received from her in response was something I'll never forget. No shame. No judgment. Just love.

Four days later I learned Dusty was safe, although she suffered a broken leg. I called Jason, and he listened to me sob. I met Craig at the doggy hospital, and he sat with me for hours. Shelli also came for support, while again, I cried. Do you see a theme?

Even though I am the one who fostered Dusty, my sister adopted her. Dusty is the happiest dog I've ever met and I'm thrilled to be her "fun aunt."

Always and Furever is rare. The people here believe in their mission wholeheartedly and will do anything in their power to save the defenseless, but they do it with kindness and compassion always at the forefront.

I'm lucky to be a small part of something so big and I can't wait to see the next one thousand dogs saved.

~

(*From Mikey*)

Shortly after A&F opened, I stumbled upon a post requesting a freedom ride for some dogs from Wichita. I had the day off, owned a big old SUV with plenty of room for crates, and I like to drive. So I tried this freedom ride thing.

I was hooked from that moment on. The feeling I get when I walk dogs out of a kill shelter and on to their second chance is like no other. I've been helping out at A&F ever since.

I've done a bit of everything including freedom rides, transport coordination, vet runs, meet & greets, adoption events, fundraisers, shuttle service at events, dog food deliveries, and I currently oversee our Facebook posting.

If you've ever considered involvement with a dog rescue, take the plunge. You can give as much or as little of your time as you want, and there are all kinds of roles to fill. Plus, the experience gives back so much more than you put into it. It gives you a sense of purpose and community.

Sure, there are heartbreaking moments and stories that make you cringe. But there are more moments that restore your faith in humanity. Dogs make us more humane. A&F's underdogs model for us how to love unconditionally, persevere through hardship, and experience a lust for life.

Thank you, Jen and everyone at A&F for allowing me to be a part of the magic of the Little Red Barn. Happy second anniversary. Here's to many more!

(From Jen)

So this is me—Jen. The good morning greeter/feeder (and sometimes evening filler inner). I'm like everyone else. Okay, not really. I prefer dogs over people 24 hours a day, 7 days a week. My social skills are nonexistent, and if I had the choice to be in a large crowd or to hide in the corner with an aggressive dog, I'd choose the dog every time.

I never thought my life would turn out this way. I don't know if anyone's life actually turns out how they planned, but I've learned to just go with it. If you don't like your life, you're really the only person who can change it.

Not much in this world scares me, so starting and running a senior dog rescue when I knew nothing about it (and had a dog-aggressive dog in my home) didn't stop me. I figured what's the worst that could happen? I'd go into extreme debt, lose everything, have no money, and fail miserably. Been there, done that.

What I've learned in the past few years is that some of my greatest achievements have all emerged from life's most painful lessons. And I know enough to know that I'll never know everything. So I don't let lack of knowledge ever stop me from doing something. I'm willing to learn, and my team is willing to learn, and that's what we do. We dive into the deep and instead of drowning, we learn to swim.

I've shared my story before, so no need to share it again. Anyone can do what I did. There was no magic — just a lot of hard work, commitment and sacrifice. If you boil it down, I am just a person who bought a farm, renovated a barn, and loves animals.

I think many are drawn to the Little Red Barn because it's real. Every person, pup, post, story, experience, is all based on the life we live and how we interpret it.

I guess we'd say we're different because we're honest about being human. Sometimes we make tragic mistakes, but maybe that's why we're not your average shelter. Although other reasons exist too, like the couches and dog beds and night night videos....

I can never put into words what Always & Furever means to me, not only the animals but the people.

I've always believed we have a choice in life, to find the good or focus on the bad because whichever one you look for will always be there. Before Always & Furever I had been in a dark place of loss and almost lost all hope. If anyone has ever lived in a place of such pain, they know that life without hope isn't a life at all. I never wanted another person or animal to feel that way, so..... insert the Little Red Barn and all the amazing people who literally help save lives.

The bottom line is that A&F isn't about me or what I did, it's about what everyone has done by coming together for their love of animals. The people who believe all souls matter and furry friends are family, not property.

Dogs are not our whole lives, but they make our lives whole.
~ Roger Caras

PART TWO
SENIOR DOG RESCUE

The dog lives for the day,
the hour, even the moment.
~ Robert Falcon Scott

ADOPTING A SENIOR

SENIOR DOGS ARE OFTEN OVERLOOKED at rescue facilities. Some believe seniors are sickly, require many vet visits, and have little time left to live. These are misconceptions we wish to overcome.

The advantages of adopting a senior far outweigh any of these concerns. While seniors *may* have a short time left, the truth is no one can predict how long any of us will live. Some seniors live well into their teen years with an excellent quality of life.

- Senior pets are typically house-broken and no longer have the desire to chew everything in sight. Dog-proofing the home for a senior pet is often unneeded.
- Many senior pets also come trained in other skills such as: sit, stay, and shake. And despite the popular saying, you CAN teach an old dog new tricks.
- While senior dogs enjoy daily exercise, they also take several naps throughout the day. They are fond of long evening snuggles on the couch. In short, they are less demanding than younger dogs.

- Seniors instinctively know you saved them. You are their hero, so they constantly desire to express their gratitude and love.

We must remember that dogs, like people, have a wide range of personalities and temperaments. Some will assimilate into a family with ease. Others may take more time to adjust. The Rule of Three makes a good barometer:

It typically takes a rescue dog...

- Three days to decompress
- Three weeks to understand and know your routine
- Three months to feel at home

A bit of patience and a lot of love goes a long way to helping these dogs become vital members of the family.

Opening up your life to a dog who needs a home is one of the most fulfilling thngs you can do.
– Emma Kenney

WHERE WE FIND OUR DOGS

To FIND good candidates for The Barn, the Intake Coordinator works closely with Jen to evaluate dogs from shelters, pounds, and even pet owners. Initially, the primary criteria included friendly senior dogs. But today, younger pups and even dog-selective dogs are considered. Our mission is to help in any capacity. Money is never a consideration.

We are part of an amazing network of like-minded people that exists across the United States. Everyone works toward the same goal: to search for willing and able rescues. Once one is found, we transfer the dogs to that location.

The Barn also works closely with a few local shelters. We closely monitor the euthanisia lists on a minute-by-minute basis. Once we identify dogs as a good fit for The Barn, we immediately tag them as safe. Often we have just a few hours to respond.

In addition, owners sometimes bring their dogs to our attention — or family members of an owner who can no longer care for a beloved pet. They have heard of our dedication to senior dogs and know the dog will be well-cared for until we find a suitable furever home.

Sometimes we hear of dogs in need from area vets. Typically, the dog is sick (or simply old) and the treatment too expensive. Rather than put the dog down, the owner surrenders to the vet, then the vet contacts us. We immediately begin a Fundme campaign to help pay for the treatment.

Unfortunately, there is no shortage of abandoned pups who need our help.

Dogs. Once they love, they love steadily, unchangingly, till their last breath.
– unknown

POUND CONNECTIONS

ABOUT A YEAR AFTER OPENING, The Barn became aware of another rescue opportunity.

While most small towns do not have the means to support a local pound, this rural community set up a small shed in the middle of the country. It housed about sixteen dogs and twelve cats but was in desperate need of help. We saw an opportunity to step in.

Lots of volunteer hours and elbow grease helped clean the cages, floor, and spruce up the building. We now maintain sanitary conditions with regularly scheduled cleaning parties. We stock dog food, cat food, and all the necessary items to ensure proper care of the animals. We have a Pound Coordinator and one part-time assistant, who offer structure and stability to these animals' lives.

Every morning the Pound Coordinator visits the facility to ensure all animals are fed, loved, and doing well. Dedicated staff walk the dogs, morning and night, 365 days a year. Even in the dead of winter, they wear head lamps for light and drudge through the snow.

No sacrifice is too great when you love what you do.

Pound adoptions follow a protocol. When a new dog or cat arrives, we share a photo on the pound's website, hoping to reconnect them with their owners. If they are not reclaimed in a week's time, these animals become part of the Always and Furever family. At this time, we schedule vet appointments. Waiting these few days ensures we do not repeat medical treatments or vaccinations.

After a seven-day stray hold, the dogs and cats are available for adoption. We complete all their vetting needs, and they become active on our Adoptable Pets page, as well as the PetFinder website. We continually promote them to help find the best placement homes. We post daily videos of the dogs and cats, hoping they will either reconnect with their original families, or connect with a new forever one.

Someday we will build another Barn — another shelter for the forgotten and unwanted. Until then, we will clean for them, walk them, raise funds, provide food, and most importantly, provide unconditional love.

BONO

(As told by Briana)

Working at the pound is not for the weak.

We see these animals at the beginning – the life before Always and Furever. Some dogs come to us growling, cowering, and afraid. Then we see an amazing transformation.

This is Bono's story.

Bono sat in the far back kennel, the one with the burnt-out light bulb. He was a big boy, his hairless feet sticking out from under the cage door. Bono's thick skin hung loose and was full of sores, almost like an elephant's hide. Yeast infected his entire body. His goopy eyes blocked his vision.

My heart broke.

Bono is probably a Pyrenees mix. He should weigh over 100 pounds. When he came to the pound, he was under 70 pounds.

He was rushed to the veterinarian's office where I visited him weekly. He was such a fighter and a true sweet heart. And oh, so hungry. He walked great on a leash, though not long distances due to his physical weakness.

Slowly Bono started to improve. A month and a half after coming into our care, he weighed 84 pounds.

Despite his abusive past, Bono holds no grudges. His tail wags the moment he sees a visitor. He only wants to snuggle in for lots of scratches and pets.

Bono is now in a foster home and thriving. He is gaining weight — and hair! He will no doubt find a furever home soon — one that will help him forget his past and embrace a bright future.

BRIANA'S STORY

Briana's Story

(Intake, Pound and Community Events Coordinator)

Our family first became involved with Always and Furever when I saw Jen's Facebook post. She asked for help to build a set of stairs for the attic Suites. I immediately volunteered my husband.

We came to the Sanctuary on a Saturday morning and instantly fell in love. I will never forget the moment we walked inside. Jen warned us to stay away from the dog named Bernadette. She was blind and a little grouchy. But Bernadette was also a perfect senior lady who became my best friend. She was the flame that ignited our passion for The Barn. Some people feared Bern, but I loved every bit of her. A picture of her hangs in my living room.

Little did we know but we had found a purpose as a family. We started coming to The Barn every day — often twice a day. After all, we had to check out the new pups. We walked the dogs, took them on car rides, allowed them to indulge in ice cream, bubbles, sprinklers, and pool time. We also helped in the evenings with dinner. It was one of our best summers.

Back then we thought we would save only nineteen dogs at one time. Then September came around. The Barn became licensed for fosters and adoptions, which attracted even more people. It has been an honor to watch The Barn grow and develop so quickly.

We soon took on fostering as a family. Jen frantically called me one night at 10:00 p.m. because Sophia would not settle. "She just keeps pacing!"

I immediately drove out to The Barn to pick her up. We instantly fell in love with Sophia, and she is still with us today. We consider her our Golden Girl.

We have fostered many pups since: Scooter, Jack, Betty, Chelsea, Wendy, Hercules, Mavis (foster failed), and Hercules #2. Now, we even foster cats.

We opened our hearts and homes to these seniors and received so much more in return. We have grown as humans and learned through all our experiences, both happy and sad ones.

The first time we had to euthanize a dog at The Barn was due to an untreatable illness. I mentally battled to let my children attend. They loved this sweet pup. Ultimately, however, I let them decide, and they wanted to be there.

Through that experience they learned life's most valuable lesson: if you truly love anything you see it through to the end. They understand it is an honor to love these animals in life and beyond.

I have been a part of Always and Furever almost since the beginning. I started as a volunteer, then transitioned to the Foster and Adoption Coordinator. Now I work with Jen as the Intake and Pound Coordinator and with local cities as the Community Event Coordinator.

Everyone at The Barn has now become our second family. It is a true blessing and privilege to get up every day and change a life. I look forward to many more days and years at The Barn.

COMMUNITY EVENTS

Briana is also our Community Events Coordinator, a role she thoroughly enjoys because "I can promote A&F to the public and build relationships."

Building meaningful community includes bringing groups to The Barn, as well as taking the dogs to local events.

These senior dogs adore visiting area nursing homes and senior centers. Since the energy levels are about the same, there is no fear of rambunctiousness. The dogs happily sit for gentle head pats and ear rubs. Or they simply lie down next to the couch or wheelchair. The residents enjoy the unconditional love and welcome the company. It is a win-win combination.

The dogs have also "marched" in local parades, visited police stations and fire departments, and attended several adoption events throughout the metro area.

Local small groups can also schedule time to visit The Barn. We have welcomed scouting troops, middle and high school students, and even an adult book club. While some education and training take place, these gatherings primarily focus on loving the dogs.

One of the more special relationships we have built is through a developmental disability organization. During non-COVID times, the residents visit The Barn once a week, typically on a Friday. Some of them help with chores. Some snuggle with the dogs and tell them stories. Some just observe from a comfy couch. The dogs love the attention, and it is a great way for all of us to end the week.

We thoroughly enjoy sharing The Barn with these groups. Children relish the opportunity to walk the dogs through pastures, do chores in the garden, bathe and brush the pups, fold the laundry, or just hang out on the sofa. Magic happens when people and dogs gather together at The Barn. We hope everyone has the opportunity to experience this paradise for themselves, at least once.

Everyone is taught that angels have wings. The lucky ones of us find they have four paws.
~ unknown

FREEDOM DRIVES

FREEDOM DRIVES REFER to the transportation of animals from a sad, often hopeless situation, to their happy ever-after locations.

At Always and Furever, these freedom drives often take place between a shelter in Wichita and The Barn. The distance is about 175 miles one-way. While this is the most common scenario, we do not limit freedom drives to this itinerary. Drives take place anytime and anywhere a pet is in need... or they find a furever home. We've had dogs find their perfect family as far away as Pennsylvania and California. No distance is too great to help these puppy dreams come true.

Several volunteers help with transportation, but because we rescue numerous dogs each month we needed a Freedom Drive coordinator. We found our rescue angel in Craig E. back in May 2019.

CRAIG'S STORY

Craig's Story

(Freedom Drive Coordinator)

I LOVE BEING A FREEDOM DRIVER!

It is a gratifying experience to go into a shelter to rescue pups, many times from death row, and start their journey to a new and better life. For others it may be sad situations of an owner who can no longer care for them because their lives are turned upside down.

So many times when you first meet these pups they are paralyzed with fear and have lost all hope. It always breaks my heart to see them so defeated and broken, not knowing what the future holds.

But then I witness their amazing transformation as they realize life is about to change. I see the hope coming back into their eyes and their demeanor changes.

For some it happens when we first greet them with a comforting voice, a smile, and a gentle hand that reaches out to let them sniff and then softly scratches an ear or neck. For others it may be as they exit the building and feel grass under their feet and the sun on their face, or when we start their freedom ride.

I always play soothing music in my SUV and tell them how their life will change. I tell them stories about life at the Always & Furever Little Red Barn and how they will be loved and cared for by staff and volunteers. I talk to them about our commitment to find them a foster or furever family who will love them, care for them, and provide them a home where they will feel safe and happy and have a wonderful life.

Being a freedom driver has been a life-changing experience for me as well. I feel so blessed to become a small part of each pup's life as they start their journey to a new, wonderful life.

Yes, sometimes it will break your heart, but so many more times your heart will soar.

DAVID'S STORY

David's Story

(Freedom Driver)

Always and Furever came into my life when I needed it most.

My life had recently changed for the worse. To say I was lost would be a major understatement. I was a rudderless ship. Then one day my mom told me about a Facebook post she had seen about a new senior dog sanctuary. They were looking for volunteers, which I thought I could do a few times a month. At first I wasn't sure how I could contribute, but eventually the answer presented itself.

A&F posted on its Facebook page a need to bring a dog from Denver to The Barn. Since I was going to Colorado the following week, I volunteered to bring Hercules back to Kansas with me. Through that experience, I realized how much I enjoyed the freedom rides. I then volunteered to go to Wichita to rescue dogs from the shelter. My involvement only grew from there.

Eventually I started my own small business focusing on animal transportation. I've made long-distance freedom drives for A&F to St. Louis, Texas, Louisiana, Georgia, Alabama, Tennessee, Ohio, and Pennsylvania. When I'm not doing long hauls, I've started helping with vet runs around town for all the pups. It's because of Always and Furever that I've been able to do what I enjoy.

The Little Red Barn is not an ordinary rescue. Not only does it save the lives of so many "broken" dogs, it's also a lifeline for people. It gave me a purpose again and a direction in life. And if I can spend my days with dogs, then that's just the icing on the cake.

Such short little lives our pets have to spend with us, and they spend most of it waiting for us to come home each day.
~ Josh Grogan

VETTING AND ASSESSMENT

ONCE A DOG IS TAGGED by A&F, and brought safely to The Barn, we then begin vetting and assessment. Occasionally, dogs we tag are in such bad shape they need to visit the local vet while waiting for their freedom ride.

All dogs receive veterinary attention, usually within three days of arrival. They are vaccinated, tested for immediate health issues, and micro-chipped. Many arrive with skin issues because of poor treatment or prior flea infestation. Other common ailments include UTIs, ear infections, and heartworm.

Sadly, the majority of the dogs arriving at The Barn need to be spayed or neutered. This is a major expense for A&F. With the seniors, there is also a large population of arthritic dogs and issues due to prior neglect, so the vet bills add up. Jen strongly believes we need to treat each dog as if they are our own, which means sparing no expense if a dog is injured, sick, or in pain. We are definitely not the average animal shelter, as it usually surprises vets the level of quality care we expect for every dog in our care.

We regularly use about three or four different veterinarians, but when the need arises, we reach out to specialty clinics. Sadly, we have many occasions where we need immediate emergency care, and we are fortunate to have a network we can count on.

We are constantly searching for the perfect combination of discounted rates (since we have so many dogs in need) plus quality care (which is of utmost importance to us). We have a team of vet runners who help us transport the dogs to the various clinics. Currently, we schedule about ten appointments a day, each round trip visit ranging from 3 to 60 miles.

Ideally, our drivers go into the clinic with the dogs. They reassure the dogs, show them love, and develop a personal relationship with each one. Unfortunately, in this time of COVID, vet appointments are curbside drop-off only, but drivers remain in the parking lot. We want to maintain as much consistency for these deserving dogs as possible.

Each new dog we take in not only receives a thorough medical examination but also a behavioral assessment. We try to learn as much about the dog's background as possible, but sometimes that information is lacking or even non-existent. Since The Barn is an open-environment, the safety of *all* dogs is our top priority. Slow introductions are essential and volunteer or foster parent observations are critical.

Some dogs are friendly from the beginning and assimilate well into the pack. Other dogs are a little more shy or uncertain of this new environment. They remain in kennels inside The Barn for a couple of days where they can observe their environment without distraction. Initial introductions take place with the new dog on a leash. The trainer monitors personal space violations while allowing the traditional getting-to-know-you sniffs.

While all shelter dogs have experienced some trauma, some bring extra baggage. Some dogs are relaxed all day except at mealtime. They must be fed in a kennel (or away from others) to avoid food aggression. Some dogs are friendly toward women but aggressive toward men. Some are non-reactive to opposite-sex dogs but aggressive toward same-sex dogs. Some were bred for hunting and therefore instinctively go after smaller breeds or cats. Some are skittish of sudden movements and/or don't know their own strength, which makes them less suitable for a household with young children.

We believe all dogs deserve a furever home. But not every home is suitable for every dog. Our responsibility is to learn about each individual pup so we can find them that perfect home where they can experience unconditional love and acceptance.

One reason a dog can be such a comfort when you're feeling blue is that he doesn't try to find out why.

~ unknown

JUDY'S STORY

Judy's Story

(Vet Run Coordinator)

I grew up on a farm, so I always knew I would do something with dogs after I retired.

In early 2018 a friend told me about her neighbor who was building a senior dog sanctuary. I stalked the Facebook page and watched her convert the horse barn into The Little Red Barn. Jen's audacious dream seemed to be just what I was looking for.

Those first few months we were only a few volunteers. I would come out twice a week and wash dog dishes, pick up poop, catch up on laundry and love the dogs. Many times it was just the dogs and me — and the peaceful Barn.

As the dog population grew (and so did our mission) there was a greater need for vet visit drivers. I found my niche. I loved getting to know the dogs on vet runs, and I enjoyed getting to know the staff at each vet office.

In two short years we grew from four-to-five vet visits a week to sometimes ten-to-twelve visits in a day! And we used an entire team of vet runners willing to drive hours every day.

Soon, I had a specific car dedicated only to vet visits — at the request of my family who refused to ride in it. The online vet calendar is now the last thing I look at each evening and the first thing I review every morning.

The dedication of A&F to provide the very best care for every dog translates to literally thousands of miles driven, massive vet bills, and a rollercoaster of emotions. We see dogs blossom and find wonderful homes. And we cry with dogs as they leave us.

What has The Barn brought me?

A community of people I would otherwise never have met who are now wonderful friends.

Three dogs (and counting) in my extended family that I never intended to keep.

I laugh out loud more than I ever have.

I cry more than I ever thought I would.

I believe strongly in Jen's dream and her uncompromising stubbornness that we can do this.

The Barn has given far more to me than I can ever give back.

All dogs are therapy dogs.
The majority of them are
just freelancing.   ~ unknown

BONDED PAIRS

A BONDED pair refers to the strong connection between two dogs that, if separated, could cause extreme anxiety, unhappiness, or failure-to-thrive.

While we most likely think of these pairs as having familial bonds, litter mates or a mom and her pup, bonds can form between unrelated dogs if they have lived together for most of their adult lives.

Always and Furever commits to keeping bonded pairs together. While a two-for-one adoption may take longer because of a few misconceptions, we know it is the right thing to do.

The truth is, these bonded pets are not twice the work. They help one another settle into a new environment. Their familiar relationship eases some separation anxiety that other rescues may experience when first arriving at a new home.

In addition, both dogs understand one another. They know how to play together, how to give one another adequate space, and how to share food and other toys. They keep one another company when the house is empty.

And bonded pairs provide twice the love and companionship.

A dog is the only thing on earth that loves you more than he loves himself

~ Josh Billings

RILEY AND ROYAL

RILEY AND ROYAL came to The Barn in June 2019. Their owner could no longer take care of them and surrendered them to our care.

These two are brother and sister, although not litter mates. Riley is a ten-year-old black male lab/chow mix who enjoys nothing more than to lie at the feet of a loving person. Royal, a seven-year-old black female lab/collie mix adores roaming the backyard. Both are as sweet as can be. We couldn't understand why they had to wait so long to find their furever home.

After patiently living with The Barn gang for nearly eight months, an experienced foster took them home. In Kristin's words:

"This sister/brother pair is amazing. If you've ever thought about having a dog, let me tell you, having two is wonderful. And finding two that are already bonded is a dream. They play with each other, sleep together, and keep one another company when you're gone. There's no adjustment period to getting along, no fights over food, and no issue with dominance."

Two short months later, Riley and Royal found their furever home. They have now completely acclimated to their new family.

"Today marks four weeks that Riley and Royal joined our family. They are now content to relax off-leash and simply lie in the yard. Initially, they were too busy looking for our barn cats. And our young daughter, who was once scared of dogs, now loves petting them and insists she be the only one to feed them."

We are so happy for Riley and Royal. The perfect family was most definitely worth the wait.

No matter how little money and how few possessions you own, having a dog makes you rich. ~ Louis Sabin

MACON AND MARLEY

MACON AND MARLEY HAD A LONG, difficult past. Like Riley and Royal, this brother and sister duo were mid-sized black dogs. For reasons we don't understand, people are less likely to adopt black dogs. Unfortunately, these two sweet ten-year-old pups spent over two years in a Georgia shelter before we tagged them as safe.

David conducted the long freedom drive. He said the only hiccup was the three failed escape attempts along the way. They arrived at The Barn around the first of October.

They assimilated quickly into our routine. Both dogs were housebroken, good with children of all ages, and fine with the other dogs in The Barn. Macon, however, thought all food belonged to her, so we learned to kennel her at mealtime. Marley took a while to warm up to men, but once trust was earned, he became a true friend. Both enjoyed snuggles, kisses, and a few gentle nibbles.

Macon and Marley found a kind foster to take them in for the holidays. They quickly adjusted to a loving home life. A few weeks later, they found their furever home. These two are now spoiled rotten and have several young children to love on them every single day.

Happy tails in a furever home is what we're all about.

There is nothing truer in this world than the love of a good dog.

~ Mira Grant

THE TWEEDLES

HENRY AND JAKE (A.K.A. The Tweedles)

These sweet "low riders" stole the hearts of every A&F volunteer.

While they were both around ten-years-old, each had a puppy face and an energetic personality. Unfortunately their backstory, such as we know it, was heartbreaking.

Locals found them. They had lived outside a marina in Missouri for over a month. We believe they somehow lost their home, and after being bounced around from relative to relative, they were completely abandoned. Folks at the marina said they often roamed the streets together and were non-reactive with other dogs they met. If any stranger offered them scraps of food, they sweetly accepted.

But as summer ended, and the marina planned to close, these two pups needed a warm, safe place to rest. How could we say no?

When they first arrived at The Barn, they had to learn the rules of the house. It took a while, but eventually the doggie diapers were no longer needed and they learned to do their business outside.

Jake was the more outgoing of the two. He never met a stranger and would completely smother you with kisses, if you let him. Henry was more of an introvert. He would often kennel himself when he felt overwhelmed. Henry was also our escape artist. That boy would outrun the fastest volunteers.

These two were always together. They knew they could trust one another, and they knew they could count on one another. What one didn't think up, the other did. We quickly began to refer to them as Tweedle Dee and Tweedle Dum — or the Tweedles for short.

While they were only at The Barn a few short months, they quickly became part of our extended family. Fortunately for them, however, their Christmas wish came true, and they found their furever home — just in time for the holidays.

They now live in the country with lots of land where they can freely run and play. Their new mom and dad spoil them daily with plenty of good food, lots of squeaky toys, and complete unconditional love. In fact, they now have an air-conditioned doghouse where they can rest and cool off while the parents garden.

Good for you, Henry and Jake. You deserved nothing but the best!

BOARDING PUPS

WHEN WE TAG a dog to bring to The Barn, we often know little about its past. While we try to find out as much as we can, it's impossible to know everything.

Our open living environment is not right for every dog. Sometimes we discover a dog doesn't do well with smaller dogs, or male dogs, or just nineteen other dogs. Sometimes they aren't dog friendly at all. Or we learn the dog doesn't do well around small children. Or they are just too young to be running around a bunch of seniors at The Barn.

Once we realize The Barn is not a suitable fit, we try our best to immediately place the dog into a loving foster home. However, that is not always possible, especially for dog-reactive dogs.

We must remove them from The Barn. So we have created relationships with a couple of boarding facilities around Kansas City. These are facilities we trust to love and care for our dogs. Boarding saves these dogs' lives.

Our volunteers regularly visit these dogs. They walk the dogs, take them for cheeseburgers and pup cups, and always love on them. Our goal is to find them a suitable home as soon as possible. Sharing social posts and pictures of our boarding dogs is one of the best ways to accomplish this goal.

AMY'S STORY

Amy's Story

(Boarding volunteer)

I discovered Always and Furever in the summer of 2018 while scrolling through Facebook. I came across the post of a beautiful male dog named Hank. While I had never heard of A&F, I knew I needed to meet this boy.

After doing a bit of research, I quickly reached out to set up a time for a tour. My sister came with me. I spent an hour cuddling Hank while Gump claimed my sister's lap. I was the only volunteer who met Daisy, and we had a great bonding experience driving to Dallas.

I am a realtor and make it a habit of donating money to an animal rescue each time I have a closing. I had a good month that summer and donated all the proceeds to A&F.

At the time, I had a beautiful Bernese Mountain senior rescue dog who was slowing down. Bernie had some health concerns, but we loved him and took care of him the best we could. It boggled my mind that someone could just say goodbye to a pet before it was time. It broke my heart that not every senior dog experienced the same love as Bernie.

Ever since Bernie, I have been involved with A&F. Since my schedule is erratic, I volunteer wherever I can. Lately, however, I've spent quite a bit of time with the boarding dogs. While none of the volunteers play favorites, I formed a special bond with Trevor. This sweet puppy had acute anxiety and easily became overstimulated. I ran with him several times a week, while another volunteer frequently took him on car rides.

As Trevor's confidence increased, I grew to love him more. One of the most satisfying experiences in my rescue life was to witness Trevor immediately fall in love with his new furever mom.

Always and Furever absolutely changes dogs' lives. Just ask Trevor.

TREVOR

TREVOR'S STORY

(As told by Amy, his boarding handler)

Animal control picked up Trevor in Wichita when he was around eight months old. While we know little of his history, he apparently had some incident with the animal control officer. We also believe a male abused him.

Since A&F is a senior sanctuary, Trevor was too young for The Barn. He went to boarding instead. We transferred him to another rescue that works with puppies. Unfortunately, we sent our biggest and tallest male to transfer him. It did not go well. Trevor was extremely scared, got worked up and eventually tried to attack the driver. The rescue refused to take him.

Trevor went back to boarding but struggled. He had acute anxiety and was losing his fur. When we took him to adoption events, he became overstimulated and would then growl, nip, or even lunge at people (mostly males).

Several of the volunteers and boarding employees created a plan to help Trevor. We took him out of the principal boarding area and put him in a quieter room to sleep. Every morning Trevor spent time outside his kennel and ran freely throughout the facility.

Soon we found a dog that matched Trevor's energy level, and they learned to play together. I ran with him several times a week, and another volunteer frequently took him on car rides.

Slowly but surely his confidence grew, and he became an amazing dog. While he still needs lots of chances to release puppy energy via runs, walks, and trips to the park, he thoroughly enjoys car rides! He has learned to sit, shake, and stay.

Trevor still deals with some stranger danger and he will bark. He does better if he initiates the meeting rather than strangers rushing up to him.

He is such a lover and cuddler to those he loves.

Trevor's Story

(As told by Lexie, his furever mom)

I adopted Trevor on January 7, 2020. I had just recently moved into an apartment by myself and was missing a canine companion. My mom had a close friend who volunteered at The Barn, so she followed the Adoptable Pets Facebook page.

One day Mom sent me a screenshot of Trevor with the caption, "Trevor did great at a meet and greet, but still needs a forever home." I instantly completed an application and anxiously awaited a reply.

It didn't take long for Tricia to reach out to me and schedule a meeting with Trevor. I met him the next night and instantly fell in love. I hadn't planned on taking him home that night because I had nothing ready. But Always & Furever provided all that I needed. I cried happy tears the whole way home. I kept thinking about his story, and how I would spoil this pup for the rest of his life.

When I brought Trevor home, he had to sniff everything in sight and check out all his new stuff. Later that night when we went to bed, Trevor crawled right up to me. I knew in that moment I made the right choice.

Having Trevor in my life has brought so much warmth and light. I find such joy in watching him learn a new trick, playing with Frisbees, going on afternoon walks, and snuggling up on the couch. Watching Trevor learn to be a dog and seeing him accept love and live life to its fullest is what makes it all worth it.

When I adopted Trevor, I knew I would bring home a dog. What I didn't know is that this dog would quickly become my best friend.

Acquiring a dog may be the only time a person gets to choose a relative.
- Mordecai Siegal

RAINBOW BRIDGE

THE 1989 MOVIE, *All Dogs Go to Heaven*, voices what all loving pet owners believe. In fact, a popular social media meme leads us to believe God has a special relationship with our beloved pets:

Kindly the father said to him,

"I've left you to the end.

I've turned my name around and have

Called you Dog, my friend."

Rainbow Bridge is that imagined place where pets go to wait for their owners so both may travel to heaven together.

Rainbow Bridge leads to an interim doggy-paradise filled with temperate sunny days, lush green meadows, and clear cool lakes. A place where dogs no longer experience sadness or pain. Where bacon treats abound. And where senior dogs can once again romp like puppies.

The front of The Barn faces west. Six floor-to-ceiling windows span the width of the building, providing the perfect view for spectacular Kansas sunsets. And on the inside, a painted rainbow arches above the windows.

While this adds a colorful element to The Barn, it also provides a special memorial for those dogs who passed while in our care. Scattered across the wall are painted paw prints, each holding the name of a single dog who crossed the bridge ahead of us. To date, over sixty-five dogs are honored.

Some angels prefer fur instead of wings.
~ Unknown

MAYME

JANUARY 3, 2020

We didn't know a thing about Mayme's personality when we tagged her from a kill shelter. We simply knew because she was sick, they locked her in a room away from others and planned to euthanize her.

Mayme's first stop was to visit the vet. She tried to bite everyone there. Then she came to The Barn and tried to bite everyone here. We knew she needed time to decompress and heal from emotional wounds. We found her a quiet spot in the loft, away from the pack of nineteen downstairs, and promised to love her through the scars. We were prepared to spend lots of time, patience, understanding and (most importantly) love to build trust. But we also knew she was worth it.

January 5, 2020

Second day here and Mayme did not bite when we put on the slip lead. Progress. Thinking about whatever she went through to feel so much pain and fear is heartbreaking.

January 13, 2020

From a dog caged, forgotten and terrified... you are now one of the pack! Our sweet Mayme. You are absolutely beautiful in this world and such a precious reminder of forgiveness and learning to love again.

January 23, 2020

Our dearest beautiful sweet Moo Moo Mayme,

It was our privilege to know you, to earn your respect, to gain your trust, and to feel your love.

Your sweet soul shines brighter than any star in the heavens. Our one wish is that all your past and tortures and pain will be forgotten and that you leave this world with only our love.

We knew from the moment we met you, we were on borrowed time and every single day with you has been a precious gift. We love you, sweet one. We love you enough to know that it's time to let you go home, peacefully, with grace, love and dignity. Tomorrow night we will say our temporary goodbye until we are all home together, once again.

Thank you for being a model of our mission. You came out of nowhere and reminded us what it means to forgive a past that was likely unforgivable. But you, sweet girl, chose love. And that's what we always strive to do. We knew, in our soul, that even if we could only give you a moment of love, we would not let you die alone.

Besides sweet girl, death isn't really the end, it's just the transition from this life to another. And the next one sweet girl.....oh my goodness! ALL our beloved friends will be there to greet you with open paws. There will be only playing and endless hot dogs. You can bite and head butt all the vets you want up there. You can shred all the muzzles. For it's only peace and love there... a million times magnified by what you felt here.

So have no fear. The angels promised us they will take care of you until we all get there and can once again hold you in our arms and feel your sloppy wet goo kisses.

God blessed us with your love.

So sweet dreams for now,

Until tomorrow,

We love you.

Always.

Furever.

You think dogs will not be in heaven? I tell you, they will be there long before any of us.
- Robert Lewis Stevenson

RHANGO

Meet Rhango our newest, youngest, littlest, and likely sickest A&F addition.

He was the runt of the litter and not growing nor keeping food down. He had a congenital issue called megaesophagus. Essentially, a major blood vessel (most likely part of the aorta) wrapped around his esophagus, preventing food from getting to the stomach. This caused him to vomit everything he ate.

Tomorrow he needs positive thoughts and prayers. He is headed into surgery to open his chest to release the vessel and widen the esophagus.

He will require a specialized diet for a long time. In addition, we need to ensure slow feeding to make sure he doesn't aspirate food and contract pneumonia. The vet may even prescribe a special chair that will hold him upright during feeding.

This surgery will be expensive. There is no guarantee it will be successful. But it is the only chance to save his little life. Rhango needs a miracle, and we know how powerful prayers are. Our entire A&F family is behind him.

You got this sweet boy. Please hold on. If you do, we promise to find you a loving, wonderful home on earth.

(The first campaign raised approximately $2120)

May 11, 2020

(The second campaign raised approximately $1375)

May 15, 2020

Our prayers for Rhango were for a long life here on earth filled with love. Maybe God's prayer was for him just to know love, even if only for a short time. But we'll never know or even understand his plan. However, during the unbearable heartache when nothing makes sense, we just have to trust it.

Here's what I do know. Every single person Rhango met, even if only online, loved him. He was sweet, innocent, pure love and a fighter. He fought so hard to live and had an army of support behind him. But today he was tired and decided it was time to leave this world. His little body couldn't survive, so he crossed the rainbow bridge to a world where he could run, eat, jump, play and do all the things he couldn't do here.

Thank you to his initial vet, who believed he was worth fighting for and reached out to us for help. Thank you to the surgeon and specialists for going above and beyond to help our little fighter. We are humbled by the love that surrounded him throughout his care. We so appreciate the prayers, the donations, and all the positive thoughts.

His life was not measured by his survival. His life will be measured by the lives he touched with love.

Run free now in heaven, my sweet friend. We all love you very much. You were worth every moment.

REX

Rᴇx's Random Acts of Kindness

(As told by Kelly, his owner)

One day a friend of mine told me about a senior dog sanctuary opening nearby. I immediately started following A&F's Facebook page and registered to attend the first volunteer training and orientation. I've been involved with The Barn ever since.

I volunteer in a variety of ways, but most often I can be found behind the wheel of a car with a dog in the backseat. We experience the freedom of cruising the streets and the delicacy of a Sonic cheeseburger.

We also fostered a dog and accepted him as a member of our family. We cuddled him, played with him, and gave him special treats. But we don't always know the backstory of these rescues. Sometimes we don't understand their triggers.

On February 21, 2019, that foster dog unfortunately killed our family dog, Rex. Obviously it was tragic and devastated all of us.

But from that experience, I wanted to do something to honor Rex's memory. He was so sweet, and so good, and (holding back tears)... we loved him.

Through Always and Furever and Sam's Devotions (another non-profit organization) I started Rex's RAOK — doing Random Acts of Kindness *for* the community and *in* the community to bring smiles to people's faces.

People email me nominations. I sort through the emails and select one specific person to receive that month's RAOK.

Sometimes I might send them a portrait of a dog they recently lost. Sometimes I might drop off dog food for their pet, or some books, or things like that.

In honor of the one-year anniversary of Rex's passing, my husband and I took the day off. We spent the afternoon doing various acts of kindness around town. We particularly enjoyed delivering fifty burgers to the shelter dogs. To watch those sweet pups devour this special treat brought us such joy.

MEMORIAL GARDEN

In the middle of The Barn's circular driveway, there lies a grassy patch of land. Pragmatically, this space helps organize traffic and parking. In reality, this is sacred ground.

In October 2018, about six months after The Barn first opened, a volunteer suggested wind chimes to honor A&F dogs who have passed on. Since prairie winds are a constant in this part of the country, the tinkling bells would be a sweet reminder of our dear furry friends. The empty space outside The Barn seemed the perfect spot.

Aline purchased the first two chimes, complete with a wooden tag that commemorates the dog's name and angel date. Currently, we have over twenty chimes in the garden, and with Alice's help and kind heart, new ones are always being added. Their soulful music greets everyone who visits The Barn. Many are moved to tears.

Six months later another volunteer suggested seating in the garden, for those who might wish to pray, meditate, or simply rest. Jan and her husband built three wooden benches and painted them yellow, blue, and pink for the colors of the rainbow.

The blank canvas soon blossomed with color. Perennials in all shapes and sizes now keep company with the wind chimes. Discarded rocks from tilling the soil now provide a heart outline for the garden. Soggy messes from an ugly drainage issue are now transformed into a white rock bed. And a wooden "rainbow bridge" now crosses that creek.

Each week several volunteers help to maintain the garden. Planting, weeding, pruning and cultivating are all acts of love for these sweet senior pups.

Dogs come into our lives to teach us about love. They depart to teach us about loss. A new dog never replaces an old dog. It merely expands the heart.

~ Unknown

JANELL'S STORY

Janell's Story

(Memory Garden)

I am blessed to be a part of the A&F Family. Who would have thought volunteering at this senior dog rescue would have such an impact on my life?

I first came to The Barn for selfish reasons. I worried about my senior dog, Jewel. I thought by volunteering I might pick up some helpful tips that would make Jewel's final years the best they could be.

I will never forget my first impression of the Little Red Barn as I arrived for my volunteer orientation in July 2019. The gentle summer breeze rang the wind chimes in what I soon learned was the Memorial Garden. As I viewed the names and death dates placed on each of the chimes, I knew this place was something special.

I enjoy working in the gardens through the summer and fall and watching it come to life each spring. I use the gifts with which God blessed me to landscape the Memorial Garden and develop its true beauty. I want the garden to honor the dogs who have passed. The gardens are a work in progress, but I can always use a good workout.

Rescue work is not for the faint of heart. It's not all fun and fluffy puppy dog kisses. I have shed more than a few tears, both happy and sad. But it has forever changed my heart. I enjoy helping these dogs find their way to a better life. And I am humbled to hold them as they cross over the rainbow bridge. As painful as that may be, it is a true privilege.

I'm a ten-year cancer survivor living with an incurable beast. Most who have my form of cancer die within five years. This is my "why."

I am blessed to work with such an amazing team, and I'm forever thankful for the many friends I've made too!

I strive to make every moment matter. For as long as I have breath, I have purpose.

BARNEY

Barney's Story

(As shared by Janell and Craig)

As a ten-year-oral-cancer-survivor, my heart hurt for this sweet boy the moment we met. I knew the pain and neglect Barney endured at the hands of those who were supposed to love and care for him.

They dumped Barney in the country to fend for himself. He was battling excruciatingly painful cancer in his jaws that eventually got so bad his jaws unhinged. He could no longer eat or chew.

During his Freedom Drive, Craig simply petted and loved this sweet boy. He tried to give him treats, but sadly, they just fell out of Barney's mouth.

Even though Barney was a part of the A&F family for just a few hours, he touched the hearts of many. We were all grateful for the opportunity to love him for that single day on earth, and we will all carry him forever in our hearts.

PART THREE

DAY-TO-DAY OPERATIONS

Dogs have a way of finding the people who need them, and filling an emptiness we didn't ever know we had.

~ Thom Jones

BARN LEAD

JEN IS the first one to check on the dogs each morning. She is up at dawn and walks across the field from her house to The Barn. She assesses the nighttime situation (any accidents — any illness — any fights) and ensures all dogs go outside to potty. She feeds the dogs breakfast and loves on them as only Jen can. She then leaves The Barn for her daytime job, and the staff takes over.

The opener arrives at The Barn around 8:30 in the morning and stays until mid-afternoon. At that time, the closer arrives and stays until 8:30 in the evening. They describe their job this way:

A typical day involves everything from love and cuddles to tears, poop, and pee. What you think will be a calm day easily turns into a whirlwind.

Our job is unique when compared to other rescues because of The Barn's open environment. The first responsibility is to keep the dogs and the people safe. To predict and avoid any fights, we constantly monitor dogs' behaviors and attitudes.

Outside the basic barn cleaning tasks (such as wiping down kennels and tending to the mountain of daily laundry) we are also responsible for a host of other activities:

- Monitor outside poop patrol
- Dispense meds
- Give baths
- Field potential foster/adopter questions
- Help with meet-and-greets
- Coordinate and help with donation drop-offs
- Organize The Barn
- Make foster and adoption goodie take-home bags
- Monitor messages from the A&F team
- Assist with emergency vet runs
- Keep track of heart worm/flea/tic preventatives
- Welcome Freedom Drive arrivals

In addition, the opener is solely responsible for the intake paperwork. Once received, the dog's medical history is then uploaded into our system.

The closer is responsible for the incredibly popular night time videos. The dogs are tucked into the sleeping spot of their choice while Jason's soothing voice assures them they are loved and will soon find their furever home.

HEATHER'S STORY

HEATHER'S STORY

(Barn Lead - Opener)

My story is a little different from others as I was not a volunteer at A&F before they hired me. I had no idea this place existed until I stumbled across a job listing for the position.

In the heat of July, Toby, my dog of eight years, went missing. I spent months looking for him every single day.

I still keep his picture in circulation and follow up on any leads. What hurts most is not knowing if he is okay, safe, and loved.

Toby is my "why." I have made it my mission to ensure that every dog who passes through this barn feels safe, loved, and wanted.

I cannot replace Toby, but I can make his absence mean something.

In the six short months I've been a part of the The Barn, I have become an expert at foster-failing. We have added two dogs and a cat to our growing herd at home. Addy was my first fail in February. She was without a doubt sent to me to help ease the pain of missing Toby. She is always at my side (even at The Barn) making sure I'm okay.

I am humbled everyday by how much our amazing volunteers do for A&F. We could not do what we do without them. I am blessed to be a part of this amazing journey.

JASON'S STORY

Jason's Story

(Barn Lead - Closer)

After fifteen years together, I lost my first rescue dog, Bridgette. Shortly after her death, I stumbled across The Barn's Facebook page. To honor Bridgette, helping these seniors became my passion.

Until I started following A&F, I didn't realize how many people abandon their senior dogs at shelters and leave them to die alone. Unlike Bridgette, these dogs aren't able to have their person with them until the end.

I followed the page for months but always made excuses to put off visiting The Barn. It was too far to drive. I didn't want to go alone.

But then I saw Brooklyn's story.

I finally found my courage to attend an Open House solo. They welcomed me with open arms, and I met some of the nicest people. Many of whom I now consider close friends and family. And I met Brooklyn. But one meeting was not enough.

I returned to The Barn for volunteer orientation just so I could see Brooklyn and the other pups whenever I wanted. I was hooked.

I started visiting all the time, doing whatever I could around The Barn just so I could be with the dogs. Mind you, I already had my own pups at home, and one of them was a senior.

But The Barn is special. All the pictures or videos in the world could never do it justice.

I started promoting Brooklyn as much as I could on my own social media. Soon, I set up my house to accommodate her special needs and fostered her. A reactive or aggressive dog can be a tough sell, so I posted about her nonstop. She couldn't talk or type, so I poured my heart out for her. I pulled at all the heartstrings to find her a great home. One month later, she was adopted. One of the most bitter-sweet goodbyes I've ever said.

That same month I joined the staff at A&F after leaving the corporate world. Literally a dream come true. I'm beyond grateful every single day. Through all the loss, heartache, bites, pain, joy and happiness, I wouldn't change it for the world.

Four little paws can change coming back to an empty house into coming home.
~ unknown

VOLUNTEERS ARE VITAL

A&F depends on volunteer support. The demands of caring for nine-teen dogs in The Barn, plus those at the pound and in foster care, are too great for one person. While financial contributions are always welcome, we also desperately need in-person help. Our mission is not only to rescue lost and forgotten dogs, but to show them plenty of loving care. An army of dedicated, compassionate people is the only way to accomplish this.

The most common volunteer duties include poop patrol and laundry. The Barn is always in a state of high-demand for these services. Of course, loving on the dogs is an absolute requirement. And we strongly encourage volunteers to take LOTS of doggie photos and post them on the A&F Adoptable Pets Facebook page. Word-of-mouth is our sole form of advertising, so these pictures literally save lives.

The more time volunteers spend at The Barn, the more they learn where their talents and interests may serve best. A few of the many volunteer areas include:

- Freedom Drives
- Vet Runs
- Dog Walking
- Dog Grooming/Bathing
- Administrative and Clerical Support
- Grounds Keeping
- Building Maintenance
- Fundraising/Marketing
- Grant Writing

If you have a special talent or skill, please volunteer your expertise. The Barn is willing and supportive of all help.

The average dog is a nicer person than the average person.
- Andy Rooney

DOGGIE DATES

In March 2020, Covid-19 shelter-in-place restrictions prevented volunteers from entering The Barn. However, the dogs still needed socialization and human affection. They needed exercise and special treats. At the same time, entire families were looking for safe social distancing opportunities to leave the confines of their home.

This mutual need resulted in a new volunteer opportunity: Doggie Dates.

We created an online schedule where volunteers could register for a one-hour Doggie Date. Volunteers drove up to The Barn at the appointed time, and a staff member walked out the dog on a leash and put him/her in the backseat of the car. A perfect no-contact pick-up.

Volunteers often took the dogs to a local park for a nice walk and then treated them to a cheeseburger and pup-cup treat. When they returned to The Barn, a staff member collected the dog from the backseat and walked him/her inside. Staff then appropriately sanitized leashes and harnesses for the next outing.

Doggie Dates became quite popular in a short amount of time. While we are hopeful social distancing restrictions will soon be a thing of the past, we may continue to provide Doggie Dates as a regular volunteer option.

You can usually tell that a man is good if he has a dog who loves him.

~ W Bruce Cameron

VOLUNTEER TRAINING

WHILE THE BARN welcomes all volunteers, we insist everyone first attend a volunteer training session. Typically, we offer these meetings one Saturday a month and they last about ninety minutes. The purpose of the training is two-fold: to educate people on how to handle multiple dogs in a confined space and to obtain a signed volunteer waiver.

These training sessions are well-attended and low-key. We encourage volunteers to find a place on the floor or a couch and snuggle with the dogs. The professional trainer provides necessary information with plenty of opportunity for questions.

Some basics covered in this session include:

- The Barn belongs to the dogs. Let them choose you. Let them roam as they see fit. Let them interact (or not). This is their space. We are guests.
- When you first enter The Barn, keep moving. Do not stop at the door because that is where territorial issues occur. Walk

slowly to a couch and take a seat. The dogs will gladly
follow.

- Do not get in the face of a dog. We do not know their past
  and therefore we are uncertain of their triggers. Pet them,
  love them, cuddle them. But don't enter their personal
  bubble.
- Be aware of dog behavior. If a dog growls, take it as a
  warning. If a dog bears teeth and/or his hair stands up, know
  he feels threatened. If a dog's tail is between his legs, he is
  frightened.
- If you feel the emotions of two dogs escalate, make a loud
  noise. You can clap your hands... yell "stop"... grab a water
  bottle and squirt them... grab a foghorn and let it rip. Most
  of these serve as a distraction and de-escalate the situation.
- If two dogs fight, do NOT try to separate them. Sound the
  foghorn and immediately herd the remaining dogs outside.

Once the session is over and the waiver signed, newbies can now
attend one session with an experienced volunteer. This is on-the-job-
training. After this first supervised session, volunteers are welcome
anytime (as long as they complete a sign-in sheet ahead of time).

The greatest fear dogs know is the fear
that you will not come back when you
go out the door without them.

- Stanley Coren

JOEY

While The Barn properly assesses all dogs before bringing them into the open-living arrangement, it is inevitable that disagreements will happen. Volunteers and staff are well-trained in spotting aggressive behavior before it escalates. Blow horns and spray bottles are valuable deterrents.

But Penny's story proved that not all Barn tales result in happily ever afters. When dealing with animals (and people) conflicts are bound to arise. Sometimes they resolve amicably. Sometimes they don't.

Here is Joey's story in Jen's words. Her kindness, compassion, and unconditional love for ALL is clear.

Like everyone, we have good and bad days at the little red Barn. Last night another dog and Joey got into a fight. All are okay, thank goodness! But to ask a dog with a past we know little about to never get annoyed or have an opinion or dislike another dog when living with eighteen ever-changing roommates is impossible.

Could you do it as a human? Why are our expectations so much higher for dogs?

We take risks at The Barn every moment of every day. We take them knowing that we cannot control or prevent 100% of the fights. We do our best to mitigate the problems, but they *will* happen.

What we can control is our response. And even when we fail to protect some or miss a warning sign, we have to remind ourselves that if we could have fixed it, we would have.

When we fail the dogs or they fail here, that doesn't mean we give up, throw in the towel, ship them away, hide them in a corner or forget about them. We find another way to help them and continue to love them. We strive to find them the right home and environment to suit their particular needs. Every dog is unique. Each one deserves a second chance.

To be honest, Joey would annoy me too. But I'm not a dog. And I don't pick fights. The other dog seemed to get along with all dogs. But his family gave him up and walked away forever. He knew that. We knew that. I wonder how many scars he carried? We must remember, however, that if these dogs were perfect they would not have been thrown away by others.

We are their second chance.

We do not judge nor condemn. We either stay true to our mission of being a model of forgiveness or we don't. I believe God is the only judge, and he calls us only to respond and react in love.

And that is what we will do here. We love both dogs, equally and unconditionally. We love Joey and we love his attacker. And we will strive to find them both furever homes that suit their particular needs.

Joey began this new year with a new furever family. Here's to a bright and prosperous future, sweet Joey!

STEPHANIE'S STORY

STEPHANIE'S STORY

(Volunteer Training)

While I am a full-time high school art teacher, I have always filled my time volunteering for different rescues. My particular focus is dog behavior.

When The Barn first opened, a mutual friend asked if I would be interested in training new volunteers at orientation meetings. At first I thought it would be twice a year, but I was amazed at the number in attendance every month.

Now, besides volunteer orientation meetings, I also help adopters, fosters, and staff. Essentially, my position is a resource for anyone associated with The Barn. I support the people and the dogs by offering dog evaluations, dog introductions, behavior modification, problem-solving specific behaviors, and preparing homes for incoming doggie guests.

Watching Jen's dream of creating this sanctuary was cool, but seeing it grow has been my favorite part. Each day I come to The Barn, I get to experience a break from everyday life and do what I have always loved: saving dogs! I can forget my worries and instead focus on one goal — to make the lives of these dogs easier.

But it doesn't stop there. This place renews my faith in humanity. We are all here for the dogs. Everyone is welcome is to be a part of this little club.

How beautiful it is to find someone who asks for nothing but your company.

– Brigitte Nicole

FUNDRAISING

ALWAYS AND FUREVER relies solely on volunteer donations. We do not charge an adoption fee because we do not feel we can put a price on saving a soul. We do not have one large contributor, but rather hundreds of committed donors. Fundraising, therefore, is essential to our rescue mission.

The Spring Gala is our biggest annual fundraising event. A dedicated team of volunteers work tirelessly for months to tie it all together. Sponsors may purchase a table for ten attendees. Individual tickets are also for sale. This is an elegant affair, so everyone dresses in their finest to enjoy a fun-filled night. A three-course meal is served along with unlimited wine or beer. And everyone bids on items in the silent auction.

We also coordinate fundraising opportunities with annual holiday traditions. For example:

- In the fall, we sponsor a *.1k Doggie Dash*. Participants pay to take part and we strongly encourage them to dress their pup in a Halloween costume.

- *Dog Photos with Santa* are a popular way to celebrate the holidays and donate to a worthy cause.
- *The Senior Doggie Bowl* is a fun warm-up activity to the Super Bowl watch party.
- A romantic *Valentine's Day dinner* with the pups was a new event this year. Volunteers served an authentic Italian dinner by candlelight as the dogs begged for a tasty morsel.

In addition, we hold impromptu events throughout the year. In 2020 we learned how to meet virtually. We sponsored a Music Bingo night and a Concoction Auction event.

We also accept voluntary donations. We regularly sponsor dog-specific GoFundMe campaigns... insisting the cost of a cup of coffee can help save a life.

On our webpage (https://alwaysandfurever.love/donate) we offer the opportunity for people to make a monthly contribution. Since vet bills are in excess of $20,000 a month, we put these donations to excellent use.

And those who shop on Amazon can support us via the Smile charity donation program at https://smile.amazon.com.

A&F merchandise is also a year-round fundraiser that serves double-duty as free advertising. We offer T-shirts, sweatshirts, baseball hats and canvas totes. Merchandise is available for sale at The Barn anytime, at in-person events, and through Facebook Message: @MarieSwartzFabrizius

SHELBY'S STORY

Shelby's Story

(Fundraising Coordinator)

I heard about The Barn two years ago when it first opened. A friend of mine, who knows my love for senior dogs, tagged me in one of their Facebook posts. About a month later, in August 2018, I went to volunteer orientation. Mama Opal was the first dog to greet me, putting her chin on my leg for pets. I was instantly in love.

My second visit to The Barn resulted in a dog sneaking out of the gate on my arrival, and I had to chase him down. I was sure they would never ask me back. Thankfully, I was forgiven.

While I have fostered around sixty animals in my lifetime, my only foster fail was Emmy Lou (ironically, the friend that introduced me to The Barn also convinced me to foster Emmy). She was mine for one week shy of three years, and she was the best dog I've ever had. Giving back to A&F helps me honor Emmy and keep her memory alive.

I soon became part of the volunteer group, where often discussions centered on fundraising opportunities. I mentioned my experience with hosting events at Hamburger Mary's. That fall we held our first fundraiser in that space. I quickly made friends with those who donated items and volunteered to help.

After this initial experience, Jen asked if I would consider organizing an annual large-scale fundraising event. After lots of brainstorming with many people, the Golden Gala was born. Even though the first year involved a lot of learning and a little crazy, we raised $30,000 with over 250 people in attendance. At our most recent Gala, we raised over $80,000!

Our fundraising success stories are truly a team effort — from the people who donate raffle items, to those who help work on-site, to those who connect us with fundraising opportunities. And we are so lucky to have amazing supporters who generously give at each event.

I'm blessed to combine my "paid job" skills of volunteer management and event planning with my passion for senior dogs. Since I am also working on a doctorate, I can't get to The Barn as much as I would like. This role gives me a way to contribute to the team.

Jen talks a lot about "no coincidences." I definitely feel that is the case of my finding A&F. It is truly my happy place. With all the ugly we see in rescue, A&F is a bright light. I am constantly amazed how gentle and loving these dogs are, even after all the trauma some of them have experienced. They are perfect examples of how we should strive to be as humans.

MARIE'S STORY

Marie's Story

(Merchandise Sales)

I've been a part of Always and Furever since the second volunteer orientation. My first night as a volunteer, I learned how to clean the floors and do laundry. I enjoyed time at The Barn so much that I started going almost every evening to help feed the dogs, give them medications, and clean.

Over time, I became more involved. I helped at events, painted a second tree on the wall of The Barn (and a few more paw prints), and made laminate signs to help organize The Barn for others. Mostly, I enjoyed hanging out, snuggling, playing with the dogs... possibly falling in love with every one of them.

My husband is a softball tournament director and my daughter plays year-round. I know from experience selling t-shirts is an excellent money maker — as well as great advertising. As The Barn's volunteer numbers escalated, I knew merchandise sales would be a good place for me to make a difference.

SPARE NO EXPENSE

Spare No Expense

(As expressed in Jen's ongoing posts)

We want the dogs no one else wants because we know every soul deserves to have a fighting chance at life — even if that time is limited. Old. Young. Sick. Abused. Weak. Strong. Crazy. It doesn't matter. Whatever issues we encounter, we do our very best to handle them.

We spend the money. We see the specialists. We do whatever we can because truthfully, these dogs are our own.

But we never charge adoption fees — EVER. And here's my reason: every single dog is a dog that someone else threw away, didn't want, couldn't care for, on death row, etc. The reason why doesn't matter. The bottom line is these dogs needed help, and no one else could help them.

We run off donations. We run off goodwill, God's pure grace, and simple acts of kindness. We live month to month, paycheck to paycheck. We have no grants. No magic big sponsors or donors or angels. We are simply ordinary people doing extraordinary things together.

We have my donations and your donations. If someone has more to give, they do. If someone has less and can only share a post or pray, that is valuable too. It's doing what you can with what you have.

So when you have a morning to skip the coffee, do it. Donate five dollars to us — or to any other rescue. All of us are in need and doing good things to help save precious souls.

Dogs are better than human beings because they know but they do not tell.
~ Emily Dickenson

WALTER

WALTER WAS a nine-year-old treeing walker coonhound. He was great with kids and large dogs, but his hunting instinct made him incompatible with smaller dogs and cats. He was a handsome fella' who crooned a hound song like no other.

Walter spent time in boarding before a temporary foster took him home for the Thanksgiving holiday. Immediately Walter accepted his new family. He spent hours roaming the wide-open backyard.

When he came in for dinner, he was tired. A few hours later, his foster mom knew something was wrong.

She immediately called Jen and rushed Walter to an emergency clinic. The vet confirmed the worst. Walter's stomach had flipped.

In the wee hours of the morning, Jen, Craig, and Kate sat weeping over Walter's fate. Jen never questioned the financial consideration. "Do whatever it takes!"

But money was not the issue. The vet worried whether Walter's quality of life, if he survived, would be greatly diminished.

In Jen's words:

We unexpectedly had to say goodbye to our beloved Walter tonight. Life wasn't always kind to this sweet boy, but his soul was always so gentle and loving.

It's easy to question God's timing. After waiting months in boarding, why did his stomach flip the day he finally headed to a loving home? He was supposed to spend years romping around the farm, exploring the pastures, and chasing squirrels. He had just found the comfort and love of a beautiful family. Why did God think one single day was enough? Why did he decide Walter's forever home would be with him in heaven instead of with us here on earth?

We'll never really understand God's plan for losing those we love, especially these souls who just love unconditionally.

Ultimately, we had to make a difficult choice. To put Walter through emergency surgery to try to save his life, despite his prior pancreatic history and dangerous liver levels? Selfishly we wanted to, but we knew Walter would suffer with little to no hope of recovery without pain.

In the end, we chose to believe God would take care of him better than we could.

Thank you, Kate for giving him the gift of a family and a home. Even for only a day, the love you gave him, the love everyone gave him, is how he left this world.

I'm so sorry, Walter, I'm just so sorry. I don't want to make the life-or-death decisions. I will never know if what I did was right. But I do know we already lost three large old pups to stomach flips. I put them through surgery trying to save them, and they suffered terribly. I didn't want you to suffer anymore. So if it was the wrong decision, please know it was at least done from love.

We both know heaven is better — so no more pain, sweet boy. We love you. Chase all the cats you want in heaven. Run wild and free and play. But please don't forget us because we'll never forget you.

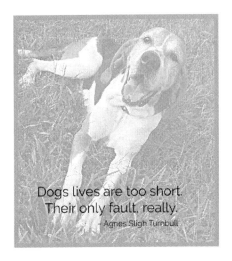

Dogs lives are too short.
Their only fault, really.
- Agnes Sligh Turnbull

LAYLA

December 3, 2019 (Kentucky shelter)

- Layla
- 5 years old
- Pitbull
- 60 lbs
- Good with dogs
- Super sweet didn't need to muzzle her at all
- She was a breeder for five years. Her owners recklessly "released" Layla and her son. Both suffered three broken legs. We could find someone for him, but no one has stepped up for her.

7:00am December 4, 2019 (Kentucky shelter)

Still no rescue offer. We cannot vet her ourselves because we cannot raise the required $5000-$10,000 needed for this major surgery. And we would still need a rescue for her recovery. She cannot stay at the shelter as she would need 24/7 supervision and we are only here eight hours a day.

So, we have decided to end her pain and suffering. Every vet we contacted told us she may be in pain for the rest of her life. They also said such a terrible break would be difficult to repair and cost thousands of dollars. We tried to raise the money but could not. She cannot sit here immobilized and in pain any longer. We do not want that for her. The best thing we can do at this point is let her go. We feel so defeated. It doesn't take long to get attached to a dog.

11:38am December 4, 2019 (Kentucky shelter)

A RESCUE STEPPED UP FOR LAYLA. Their name is Always and Furever Midwest Animal Sanctuary in KS. You can donate to them to help save this girl.

Afternoon of December 4, 2019

Meet Layla. She was hit by a car and suffered three broken legs. The breaks are complicated and expensive to repair. She found herself in a shelter in Sparta, Kentucky with just about a zero chance of adoption. If Layla didn't find a rescue today, they would let God take her pain.

Well, someday that will be the case, but that day is not today. We are tagging, bringing her here, and promise to give her a chance at a life without pain, in whatever form that may be.

Life is about to change sweet one. To be continued....

December 7, 2019

The day we learned Layla needed us, David dropped everything on his schedule and made the round trip from Kansas to Kentucky to give her a chance at life without pain, to know what it's like to be loved.

With the extensive damage to both front legs, we knew she could only see the best. We headed straight to Missouri Orthopedic Surgeons. Layla arrived safely at MU Thursday around 2:30pm. She spent the night in the ICU getting her pain under control. They completed her lab work and x-rays. Layla went to surgery about 1:00pm yesterday.

Layla has fractures of both her front humerus leg bones. A comminuted fracture is a break that goes completely through the bone. There are also fragmented pieces which makes it a more complicated to repair and heal.

After a seven-and-a-half-hour surgery, the orthopedic surgeon notified us at 10 pm that he successfully repaired both legs. They used two bone plates secured with pins to bring the fracture together and stabilize the bone. They then splint the legs so they could monitor the surgical wounds.

Layla's journey is just beginning. She must keep weight off her front legs for several weeks. This means her friendly humans will have to use a sling to help her potty and to change her kennel positions for comfort.

During this time, her muscles will weaken and her joints will become stiff. Once she is cleared to begin physical therapy, she will have to start stretching, strengthening, and learning to walk again. It will probably be a six-to-eight-month rehabilitation.

But Layla is a fighter, and we are committed to her recovery. The cost of her care will be close to $10,000 ($4,500 per leg and then medical boarding where she can receive the care and treatment she needs on her journey to a new life).

. . .

December 11, 2019

Our Christmas Miracle came through surgery like a warrior. It was another seven-hour surgery. They opted for the external fixator, which will give Layla the best chance at a positive outcome.

She is already eating well again this morning and pushing herself up in the kennel with BOTH legs. She can put weight on her left leg now with this device. She will have this external fixator for a minimum of eight weeks, so she will be in medical boarding for a good bit. She is getting stronger and stronger each day.

April 19, 2020

(From Layla's foster mom)

Layla Lou went to the vet last Wednesday, April 15, 2020. I tried to go with no expectations, but in my heart I was hoping for good news: legs healed, hardware off, something good for this precious little warrior.

Here's what we learned:

Good News: she gained 6-8 pounds and the right leg has made a little progress.

Bad News: they cannot save the left leg.

The Plan: nothing has changed — they will leave all hardware in place so the right leg can heal another two weeks with full support.

Left leg amputation is scheduled for April 29th.

They will remove right leg hardware on May 13th.

Please keep praying and sending positive thoughts. Layla has worn this hardware for 133 days and has another three to five weeks left to go. And her fight doesn't end there. She will have to learn to walk as a front end amputee and have to continue to fight the infection once the hardware is out.

A&F family, we have only come this far with your support and will only get to the finish line with your continued love.

Layla and this foster momma cannot say thank you enough.

April 29, 2020

It's official...

Layla Lou is now a three-legged Warrior Princess.

One hundred and fifty days after that stupid breeder threw her in the road like a pile of trash and left her to die, Layla lost her left leg.

But we are still not handing him the victory. Oh no! That will never happen. Layla has fought this far and will keep fighting with us by her side.

The right leg continues to show signs of improvement. Xrays show more bone growth than even two weeks ago. So, we will leave the hardware on the right leg for two more weeks to give her some support as she adjusts to being a tripod. And then she will go back to surgery on May 13 to remove the hardware.

We will also continue to fight the infection with these heavy hitting antibiotics until it is gone.

And if, for some reason, Layla's right leg doesn't want to hold her up...we will. We will carry her. We will put her in her cart and take her wherever she needs to go. We will never throw her out or give up on her because we love this little amazing dog with all our hearts. She's not trash.

Thank you A&F family for all your prayers and support!

May 13, 2020:

Well, this momma is uncharacteristically speechless.

158 days later...Layla is finally hardware free!

My little warrior can lie on the dog bed for the first time in 5 1/2 months without a piece of metal poking her in the face or having to tilt her neck in a weird way. She can finally curl up on my lap like a dog should be able to.

She is not feeling great because of anesthesia twice in the past two weeks. And she can't put full weight on her leg for at least two weeks. Plus, we are still fighting this nasty infection.

But we will worry about that tomorrow. Tonight we will hold Layla. Her sisters, foster sister, and the puppies are snuggling her. The tears of joy and blessing are abundant.

Thank you, A&F family. Without you, none of this would be possible.

PART FOUR

THE HEART OF THE MATTER

Those who teach the most about humanity aren't always human.

~ Donald Hicks

WHAT IT MEANS TO FOSTER

To DATE, Always & Furever has rescued over 1,000 dogs!

This would not be possible without our volunteer fosters.

The Barn is zoned for only nineteen dogs at a time. If we are full, we cannot rescue another until someone adopts a dog OR one of our dogs leaves for a foster home.

In essence, fostering helps save not one but two lives.

While all dogs in our care are available to foster, some are more in need than others. Our open atmosphere of nineteen dogs is not conducive for some new arrivals — especially those we fondly refer to as "the littles." They are anxious and timid. They require a quiet, calming place to decompress (and to run around without fear of being trampled by an oblivious larger dog).

Other dogs come to us with more medical needs than we can properly tend to in The Barn. They need extra time, care, and patience to mend and heal.

And some dogs come to us with lots of emotional baggage. They may get along with some dogs but not others. They may not get along with dogs but are fine with cats. These furry friends desperately need the loving care of humans who can accept them just the way they are.

Fostering with Always and Furever is an easy and rewarding process. The first step is to complete a form online at www.alwaysandfurever. love/forms.

Some considerations are necessary in choosing the right dog for the right foster home. For example:

- Does the home have stairs? We want to make sure the dog does not have arthritic issues that hinder mobility.
- Does the home have other pets? We want to make sure the dog does not have any known issues with other dogs or cats.
- Does the home have young children? We want to make sure the dog is tolerant of a child's energy level and curiosity.
- Does the home have a fenced-in yard? We've had several dogs in our care who played "Houdini" and quickly escaped if not adequately protected.

Once the foster selects the right dog, their role is simple: treat the dog as your own. We can provide the bedding, kennels, food, monthly flea/tick/heartworm treatments as well as other monthly medications. The foster provides the house and the love.

In addition, we ask the foster to promote the dog on our Facebook page, Always and Furever Adoptable Pets. The more visibility for our dogs, the better chances we have in finding their perfect family.

While we sometimes know the backstory of these rescues, often we know very little. As fosters learn the various personality traits of these dogs, they share that information online. The more potential adopters know about a dog, the better success rate in finding its furever home.

Of course, after caring for the rescue for a few days, fosters may decide they want to adopt. We affectionately call this Foster Failing. There is no shame involved in this kind of failure, only big congratulations and lots of slobbery kisses.

Blessed is the person who has earned the love of an old dog.
~ Sidney Jeanne Seward

MEGHAN'S STORY

Meghan's Story

(Foster Coordinator)

I followed A&F's Facebook page for a while, watching those good morning videos and good night videos. I had no idea I lived near The Barn.

Around the first anniversary (May 2019) I attended volunteer training and immediately became actively involved. While I've performed many roles and duties, I accepted the position of Foster Coordinator in March 2020.

What I like best about this role at A&F is the opportunity to witness these animals' transformation — from scared shelter dog to happy family pet. I am privileged to help find them a good place to learn how to live in a home and simply be dogs.

We foster approximately fifty dogs a month, so we are constantly busy. No two days are alike. I spend most of my time reviewing foster applications, making necessary verification phone calls, monitoring which dogs are coming into The Barn, and working with the adoption coordinator to keep up-to-date on those fosters who have found their furever home.

To say being a part of A&F has been life-changing is an understatement. The happiness, heartbreak, laughter, friendships, and endless hours to help save these dogs is a rollercoaster of emotions. And absolutely the best thing I have ever done.

I am blessed to be a part of Jen's dream and make a difference in these dogs' lives. It is the most fulfilling job I have ever had. The Little Red Barn not only saves animals, it saves humans too.

A FAMILY AFFAIR

FOSTERING IS a Family Affair

(As told by the Daniels' family)

About two years ago, my wife Kristin informed me that our entire family .was going to the volunteer training at Always and Furever. I have to admit I was skeptical. It was not the way I wanted to spend an hour and a half on a Saturday afternoon.

However, the moment I pulled into the driveway, I knew this place was something special. It was different: a haven for senior dogs unlike anything I had ever seen.

Volunteers immediately greeted us. Although the place was packed, they made us feel welcome. And the dogs were free to roam about the comfy couches and chairs.

Suddenly I realized how much our family could benefit from volunteering at A&F. They all worked as a cohesive team, and we all had one commonality: a sincere love for dogs. My boys would have a heyday! And my wife? She was in doggy heaven.

The training was informative, genuine, and showed the compassion that all the leaders, especially Jen Dulski, had for dogs.

Before we knew it, we were all-in for Always and Furever.

My wife was the engine behind our family volunteering, always saying, "Hey, let's go to The Barn!" She is the organizer and Facebook poster extraordinaire.

I mowed the yard in my free time—something therapeutic and enjoyable for me.

And my eight-and nine-year-old boys had the best job of all: loving on the dogs.

It was more than just serving, though. It was a way for our family to bond. To spend quality time together. We came three, maybe four times a week during the spring and summer. I took my boys on three sleepovers at The Barn, creating memories we would cherish forever.

At the end of our first month of volunteering, we all knew the next step was unavoidable. We had to foster a dog. Enter Juju, a short, squat three-year-old Bassett-Pit mix that bounded into our lives with youthful passion. This was the perfect way to experience a bit of Always and Furever at home, at no cost to us.

Two and a half months later, Juju found her forever home in Gardner. A young couple needed a bit of spice in their life and fell in love with her at first sight. That made room for Snoopy... and Angel... and Bear... Polly, Scooter, Nancy Regan. I could go on, but will stop there.

We are now on number 19: Waldo, who quickly became our first Foster Fail. Each dog's story led them to a forever home. Their memories, left behind as vivid as a bright red barn on a sunny morning, will live forever in our hearts.

Forever. What a powerful word that is — a word that has no ending. Just as it goes on and on, the love for the dogs at Always and Furever will too. I cannot think of a reason anyone would not want to become a part of this family to experience that love. Whether it be fostering, adopting, or just volunteering, there is a place for everyone.

Always and Furever.

BETH'S STORY

Another Foster Story

(As told by the Wooldridge family)

Our family has volunteered at A&F since May 2019. Our son needed community service hours for his high school Animal Health program. Who knew one little afternoon at orientation would change us forever.

We started by loving on the dogs and helping where ever needed. We especially enjoyed taking pictures of the dogs and then posting to social media. We knew this kind of exposure helped find them their furever homes.

We soon realized we wanted to do more. We attended in-person adoption events, orientations, open houses, etc. We found our passion.

However, we knew we would never EVER foster. I didn't want to deal (or have my boys deal) with the heartbreak of saying goodbye to a foster when he/she found a new home.

Well, never say never. We have now fostered eight dogs since we started volunteering. All of them have touched our hearts in ways we never knew possible. And I know we made a difference in each of their lives.

Jen says during orientation, "Fostering saves two lives, the dog for whom you provide a temporary home, and another dog who can now be saved because there is an open spot at The Barn."

In February 2020 our first foster, Klondike, crossed the rainbow bridge while in our care. It was beautiful and heart-wrenching at the same time. Klondike was a part of our family for just a few short months, but he stole our hearts and taught us what being a foster is all about.

Why do we foster? We do it for us as a family. We have learned what it means to help a cause we believe in. We do it because other humans failed these animals and we can make a difference. And we do it because we adore the unconditional love we receive from these animals.

In memory of Klondike, we will continue to foster, volunteer, share stories and photos, and work with all the other volunteers to make a difference.

HOSPICE FOSTER

Sara's Story

(Hospice Foster)

In 2018, shortly after losing a family pet, I promised myself to always help dogs. A month later I discovered Always and Furever.

I fell in love with Jen's story and mission and knew I wanted to be involved.

We adopted Priya, a cute black lab, in October and were privileged to love her for seven months before we lost her to cancer. A week later, we were back at The Barn and met Zoey, who had recently lost her bonded partner. Zoey needed time to grieve and adjust. We fostered her for fourteen months.

We could not ignore Jen's emergency call in October 2019. Raven had been chained under a porch her entire life. She had some mobility issues, and they did not think she would live much longer. Since I had recently been involved in a car accident with mobility issues of my own, I connected with Raven. While Raven is technically classified as Hospice because of an untreatable under-lying condition, she still lives with us today.

Raven was not our first Hospice dog. Three years ago, we fostered a dog from the Lawrence Humane Society. Mickey had cancer and required surgery. Unfortunately, they were unable to remove all the cancer from Mickey's muscle and gave him six months to two years to live. We brought him home, where he still lives today.

At this point, we wondered if we had a special touch with Hospice dogs. While we don't have any unique skills besides being first responders (my husband a firefighter, and I a police officer), we have cared for several dogs with a myriad of medical issues over the course of 10+ years.

And we have a lot of patience. Rescues, and Hospice dogs in particu-lar, don't always have the best manners. Many have experienced pain, abuse, neglect and abandonment. They've been let down and must learn to trust again.

So far, we have fostered four Hospice dogs in 2020. The first was Slider, whose body was basically eating itself. Jen wanted him to feel the love of a caring home and a warm bed before we had to say good-bye. Slider stayed with us for a weekend. Then my husband and I held him as he crossed the rainbow bridge.

How quickly we attach to a dog, even knowing it will be for a short time.

In May we picked up Armstrong, who had large masses in his lungs. He was given about two days to live. Week after week we nursed Armstrong, and he continued to improve. He would go for walks and was a giant snuggler.

However, the first week of September, Armstrong suffered what appeared to be a stroke. A little over a week later, he experienced breathing problems. My husband and I slept on the floor with him through the night, but his respiratory distress did not improve. The next morning we had to say goodbye.

This one really hurt. I was Armstrong's person, and I had grown attached to him in our short three-and-a-half months together.

The first week of August, while we were still nursing Armstrong, A&F's foster coordinator contacted me about another Hospice opportunity. Brownie was diagnosed with liver cancer and the cancer had spread. I picked her up that day. They did not expect Brownie to make it more than a few days. She has been with us for over a month.

The day we lost Armstrong, Jen contacted me about Zack. "I know it's too soon after losing Armstrong and "likely inappropriate" to ask, but Zack needs a soft place to land for his remaining days."

"I need the evening to grieve," I said, "but I'll be ready tomorrow."

Zack has liver and kidney cancer and probably dementia. He has been our most challenging Hospice foster because he's had little interaction with other dogs. Consequently, Zach does things to make the rest of the pack a bit uneasy.

But that's rescue. You have to learn to adjust. You have to be resilient. None of them are perfect. But none of us are either.

Several have told me I should stop taking Hospice dogs. They know it hurts me to lose them. But I see it as a privilege to love on the dogs that need the most help — the abandoned, the forgotten. Teach them to trust people again. Hold them when they don't feel good.

I also hold them when they finally cross the rainbow bridge. Yes, it hurts. Sometimes a lot. But it is always worth it.

Always.

ADOPTION: THE FUREVER HOME

A&F's ultimate goal is to find forever homes for each and every dog we rescue. A home where they will be treated as family. A home where they will find only kindness, love, and comfort. A home where they may live out their best days.

Once a dog comes into our care, we immediately vet and assess them. If needed, we will have them spayed/neutered and micro-chipped. The Barn covers all these expenses.

After the initial assessment, dogs will then come to The Barn (if suitable to that environment), or go to a boarding facility, or placed with a foster (sometimes a medical foster is required for the severely sick or injured).

We then immediately post the dog's picture to our website (www.alwaysandfurever.love/adopt-a-pup) as well as our Adoptable Pets Facebook page. Social media and word-of-mouth is our best strategy to find the perfect family.

While we strive to place every dog in a home, we take appropriate measures to ensure it is the perfect home. These dogs have endured so much — whether illness or injury, rejection or abandonment. And we want their next placement to be a stable environment.

Potential adopters must first complete an online application (www. alwaysandfurever.love/forms) where we inquire about past pet history and request a list of personal recommendations. We vet our adopters as closely as we vet our dogs.

Once we locate a suitable adopter, we arrange a meet-and-greet with the dog. This could be at The Barn, at a foster's home, or some neutral place like a local park. This gives both parties an opportunity to check each other out to ensure a perfect fit.

If we deem the match suitable, the adoption is complete.

We charge no adoption fees because dogs are priceless. How can we put a dollar-value on these precious lives?

Instead, we focus on finding the right families who are dedicated to taking care of these pets for the rest of their lives. And since we save the dogs that others ignore, this often requires a financial sacrifice to ensure they receive the proper medical attention.

Adopted dogs immediately become a part of our Facebook Alumni group. We relish seeing these old friends acclimate to their new homes, and we encourage all adopters to post frequent updates.

TRICIA'S STORY

Tricia's Story

(Adoption Coordinator)

I learned about Always and Furever on their social media Facebook page.

At the time, I was looking to foster dogs and saw that A&F rescued seniors. We had an opening at our home where we could bring dogs in and foster them.

The first dog we fostered was Zeus — a 90-pound pitbull that came in like a wrecking ball. He stayed with us about six months until we found his forever home. He was a big gentle giant but just needed time to find the right home.

We have fostered several dogs since Zeus. We usually bring the higher maintenance dogs to our home because we have the space to separate them from our pack. This allows them time to adjust to home life. We acclimate them to being in a home, being with people, sleeping in beds, and going outside.

Fostering has been therapeutic for both my family and me. We all have stories, and animals have always been a part of my life growing up. Being able to be a part of A&F now has been life changing.

After fostering for A&F for many months, the opportunity came up for me to become the Adoption Coordinator. I took over that role in December 2019 and have been going full speed ever since.

I work with an amazing team here. My job involves not only learning about the dogs, but trying to get the dogs adopted into their second-chance furever homes. I can pursue my passion and do what I love. It's the best thing I've ever done.

These dogs need us more than we know, but we also need them. They teach us so much. Fostering has allowed me to know the stories of the different dogs, as well as learn stories about myself. And I can be part of a heaven-like place.

A dog is the only thing that can mend a crack in your broken heart.

~ Unknown

INDY

A SPECIAL ADOPTION Story

(As told by Indy's furever family)

About a year ago we were looking to adopt a dog that would be a suitable match for our young daughter. Lily is diagnosed with non-verbal autism. In addition, she is characterized as Sensory Seeking — meaning she really likes hugs, kisses and being near people. We needed a dog who would be comfortable with that and wouldn't mind constant "in your face" contact. We needed a dog who would be patient and well-mannered.

In sharing this idea with friends, Kelly Driscoll, a volunteer at Always and Furever, recommended A&F as a potential place to find this dog of our dreams.

We began our search by following The Barn on social media. The first time we saw Indy's photo, we fell in love. We thought she was the most beautiful dog we had ever seen.

We then scheduled a visit to The Barn.

Jen is awesome. When we walked in it was like she knew us already and welcomed us with open arms. She's passionate about finding the dogs a home. In fact, everybody there really cares about the dogs and it's obvious the moment you step foot in the door.

We met a couple of dogs and of course we loved every dog we met. But it was most important to us to find the right match for our circumstances.

The first time we met Indy was when we fostered her for a weekend around the Fourth of July. We saw how she did, learned who she was, and we ended up never giving her back.

Indy has been everything we expected and wanted out of a dog.

WRIGLEY

Wrigley's Story

(As told by his adoptive mom)

Before Wrigley came into my life, I was still mourning the death of my basset, MaaDee. I wasn't sure I was ready for another pet.

But I saw a video on the A&F Facebook page of a basset hound in a shelter cage. He had the sweetest face I had ever seen, and I instinctively knew I needed him as much as he needed me. I believed MaaDee sent him to me to heal each other's hearts. So I applied to adopt without meeting him.

I drove four hours to get him. When he got out of the back of Craig's SUV, Wrigley came straight to me. We immediately bonded and drove off into the sunset.

Even though Wrigley lived with me only six short months, he healed wounds I didn't know I had — and some I knew needed healing. A&F not only saves dogs, they save people too.

Wrigley was a beautiful basset. I will forever remember my sweet wiggle butt. To honor his legacy, I am now giving love to another A&F adopted boy — Clifford. We are both working through our grief of losing a loved one, one day at a time.

Dogs are like that, I guess. They know how to fix you without ever saying a word.
~ unknown

HERO

Hero's Story

(As told by Hero's furever family)

We know little of Hero's first seven years of life. He has a beautiful coat, soulful eyes, and is completely house trained. He knows "Sit," always carries a lovie in his mouth, and sweeps the dog park like a well-trained hunter. In other words, we think a previous owner cared for him at some point in life. But that drastically changed in October 2019.

At that time a local television station reported two dogs were found locked in a storage unit. One a mere puppy near death. The other a large and rather vocal lab. They immediately took both dogs to the vet for treatment. After two weeks, the lab was healthy enough (and energetic enough) to go to a foster home. The puppy needed significantly more care.

Because the owner was now incarcerated, and the dogs were considered evidence, the lab could only be released to a rescue — not an individual. Enter Always and Furever.

Briana called me the week before Thanksgiving and explained the situation. "Would you be willing to foster the dog until the case is resolved?"

I talked with my husband and in thirty seconds gave her our answer: "How can we say no?!"

On December 4th we drove to the vet's office, not quite sure what to expect.

The staff greeted us with warm smiles. "You're here for the lab we call Bo. Hope you don't mind barking." The vet told us the lab greets anyone and anything that enters the office with a loud, long hello. And he especially enjoys chatting with the cow in the next stall.

Then the vet shared this story:

"A visitor to the storage facility heard barking — non-stop barking. After a few minutes they asked the manager to open the unit. What they found were two dogs. Each in a lay-down crate. Food and water at a minimum. We estimate these dogs were locked away for nearly a month. If it weren't for Bo's incessant barking, these dogs would not have survived."

We never learned his original name. The vet named him Bo. But after hearing his story, we knew he was a genuine Hero.

While I could wax on about this sweet boy, I will end with a recent event.

We took Hero back to the vet for preventive medications. The puppy (named Foxy) had now been adopted by the vet. He brought her out to see how the two would react.

Initially, they both ignored one another. But then Foxy recognized something — a scent, maybe? She went crazy! She lay down in front of Hero. She continued to jump on him and give him kisses. She could not contain her excitement.

The vet kept saying how unusual this was for Foxy. She always growled at visitors and was highly protective of the staff.

But she recognized her Hero. They share a love bond that will last forever.

And how privileged we are to witness this happily ever-after story.

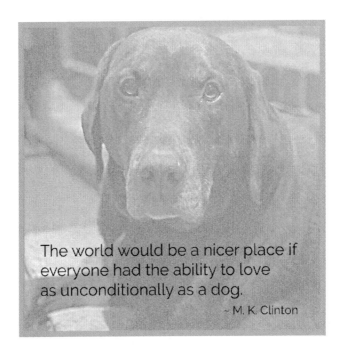

The world would be a nicer place if everyone had the ability to love as unconditionally as a dog.

~ M. K. Clinton

CALIFORNIA LABS

A LONG-DISTANCE ADOPTION Story

(as told by their furever family)

It was a Sunday in late Fall 2018. I was mindlessly scrolling through Facebook when something caught my eye. Not just any something. This something made me stop and look.

On my screen were three beautiful Labrador retrievers — all locked individually in cages at a shelter in the Midwest. The post stated the three would be euthanized unless someone rescued them. My heart broke, and I began to cry. Then I sprang into action.

I tried to reach the shelter by phone, but since it was later in the Midwest than at my home in San Diego, my call went directly to voicemail. I left a desperate plea to not euthanize the dogs and begged someone to return my call. I planned how I could drive to the shelter to pick up these three dogs I had never met. My husband pleaded for me to be reasonable, but I couldn't. That night I cried myself to sleep.

The next day I received a message stating a local rescue had collected the dogs. When I called to verify this information, I was told they passed the dogs on to Always and Furever because of their ages. I subsequently called A&F and learned these bonded girls would be adopted together. While it relieved me the girls were safe, I could not shake the memory of their faces.

I followed A&F on Facebook every day, looking for photos and information on these three girls whom they named Macaroni, Maple and Milkshake. We already had a rescue lab mix and a cat. Was it crazy to add three more dogs we had never met?

After two weeks I submitted an application for adoption, even though it felt like a dream and completely insane. While my husband was still not on board, I felt certain in my heart this was meant to be. My application was approved.

Now we had to determine the logistics of driving the dogs from Kansas to San Diego in the middle of winter with holidays approaching. I knew it would take a while. In the meantime, I continued to keep tabs on them on the A& F Facebook page. We purchased a dog door so they would always have indoor/outdoor access. We collected sheets and bedding so they would be cozy in their new home.

We knew we had time, but the excitement was building. Eventually I got the call: they had a drive train to get the dogs to us in late January. However, during their stay at The Barn, they had become friends with another lab named Lady. Would we consider taking four dogs? I said I would talk to my husband. Someone on the A&F side got excited, and posted we were taking all four. The decision was made for us!

The trip took the drivers longer because of inclement weather, but the dogs arrived around 3:30 AM on January 21, 2019. They strategically left Milkshake (now Cora) as the last one. She is HUGE and a complete goofball.

I slept on the couch that night so I could be with them in their new space. That morning our first dog, Tyra, came out of the bedroom — her face in complete disbelief. She was not happy about four strange dogs in her house. However, over the past year she has grown to tolerate them. While they will probably never be best buds, they have managed to get by.

We soon started a Facebook page for the girls so their fans from the Midwest could follow them. Fab Four Rescue Labs now has three hundred followers.

We have experienced some sadness since the girls arrived. We lost Lady in late October, and then Maple passed just five weeks later. While we know this is part of adopting senior dogs, it doesn't make it any easier.

Everyone who hears this story thanks us for saving them. I always say, I feel I am the lucky one. I truly believe with the many dog posts I see, I was guided by fate to find that post. And it has forever changed our family's lives, for the better.

GOLIATH

(As told by Jen prior to finding his furever home)

This is my friend Goliath. Every morning he greets me with a big silly yawn, and paw shakes asking for love. He then stretches out on the couch waiting for belly rubs. Goliath is around seven years old and has much love to offer.

So why doesn't he have a home when everyone desperately loves him?

Well, it's simple. Goliath was used for fighting. For that reason, he must be the only pet in the house which means no cats, no other dogs, and no tiny humans. He is very strong, and that scares people away.

Goliath is heartworm positive and going through his second treatment. He is on the road to recovery but he needs a quiet home, with only a few steps to keep the activity low. He also needs a fenced yard, someone to snuggle him on the couch and love him.

So maybe Goliath has a past, but honestly, who doesn't? We all come with scars. Some are just more visible than others. And while Goliath may carry his scars across his body for the world to see, his heart remains pure.

Goliath has issues, but no human or furry friend is perfect. He deserves a home. We'll walk you through everything. We have a trainer to talk to you and set you up for success. All we need is someone willing to accept his love, who will protect him, his heart, and his life.

So please share his photo, share his story, tag someone and show them how this sweet boy interacts. Talk to people who took him on a doggie date. Please don't dismiss him and judge him for his past. Help us change his life and build a new future with the loving family he so desperately deserves. He's waited too long.

About one month later...

Welcome Goliath — Big G — G Man, to the alumni family!

We knew yesterday when Goliath took their hands into his paws. They spent the last two days with him, and we watched Goliath work his G-magic. It was meant to be.

We are the lucky ones. Goliath blessed all our lives. This bug hunk of love taught us to stop and watch the sunset, sit and hold a paw, always enjoy a good cheeseburger.

We all love you, Goliath!

PART FIVE
SOME DOGGIE FUN

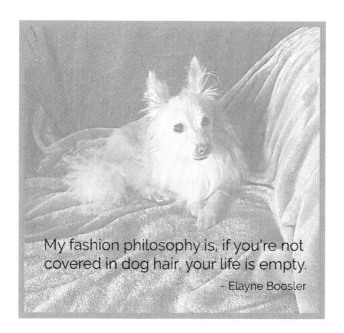

My fashion philosophy is, if you're not covered in dog hair, your life is empty.

~ Elayne Boosler

HOLIDAYS AT THE BARN

WHILE A&F is serious about saving dogs' lives, we have fun too. Especially around the holidays.

For those volunteers who are away from family this time of year, we organize a special **Pupsgiving** dinner. Furniture is rearranged in The Barn to accommodate family-style seating in the center of the room. Everyone brings a dish to share and a beverage of choice. Christmas Carols play on the sound system and relaxed conversations abound. Of course, the dogs appreciate the cuddles and any crumbs that happen to fall on the floor.

In 2019 we organized a **Dear Santa** letter campaign. Each day from Black Friday to Christmas Eve, our Facebook page featured a different letter to Santa written by one of our adoptable dogs. Each letter told a bit of the dog's story (and hinted at their personality), requested Santa bring a special gift to The Barn, and always ended with the plea for a furever home.

The letters resulted in many useful donations and several dog adoptions.

We also promoted a **Clear The Barn** campaign for the three days surrounding Christmas. We requested pick-up before December 24th, and we welcomed returns as early as the 26th. The campaign was very successful. We found temporary fosters for every single dog! This gave the dogs an opportunity to experience a real home, even if for a few days. And it allowed our faithful staff a few days off to spend with family and friends.

DESTINY

Dear Santa ~

This time last year, I was very sad. My first owner abused me — my second owner surrendered me — and my third home was a shelter that put me on the euthanasia list. That was a lot to handle in just two years of life.

Thank goodness for Jen and the Little Red Barn. Do you know her? I think she might be one of your elves.

Anyway, she rescued me and gave me a second chance. I am SO grateful.

I tried to make friends at The Barn, really I did. But my unstable past made me anxious and I didn't enjoy time with other dogs. So eventually Jen found me a comfortable spot in boarding.

But Santa, I really love The Barn. Could you bring them something special... something they need to help them help other dogs? I think some cans of spray cheese and jars of peanut butter would be perfect!

While I'm nervous around other dogs, I absolutely love humans! Male, female, young, or old... it doesn't matter. I can't get me enough one-on-one attention with lots of snuggles.

I also love car rides, long walks, and playing fetch in the yard. I have lots of fans who come visit me, and they love to take my picture. Maybe you could bring me a new toy to pose with?

I hope I don't sound ungrateful, Santa. I really love this new life. But what I want most of all is a new furever family to call my own. While I need to be the only dog, I promise to be the bestest dog they could ask for.

What do you say, Santa? Could this be my destiny?

Dogs are our link to paradise. They don't know evil or jealousy or discontent. To sit with a dog on a hillside on a glorious afternoon is to be back in Eden, where doing nothing was not boring -- it was peace.
- Milan Kundera

#BRINGLUKETOTHEFARM

Due to an unusually wet spring and summer, Luke Bryan postponed the Kansas portion of his 2019 Farm Tour until the fall. The event was scheduled to take place about thirty miles from The Barn.

A&F learned of the singer's support for senior dog rescue and started a social media campaign to invite Luke to The Barn. Jen wrote daily posts, each with a unique twist — always from Gump — and flooded all Facebook accounts. Volunteers shared the posts thousands of times.

The posts were too good not to share.

16-Oct-2019

****Share this Post*****

Help Make Gumpy's Plea Heard!!!!

#bringLuketothefarm

Dear Luke Bryan,

Gump here. You may have heard of me. I mean I'm a pretty well-known celebrity in these parts and I heard you were coming in town on your Luke Bryan Farm Tour. Since we are both kind of a big deal and constantly battling the daily paparazzi, I figured I would offer you a quiet, peaceful spot to crash at my humble abode called the Little Red Barn — otherwise known as Gumpsville. I may be the only one who calls it that but that's beside the point. I really just wanted to offer you a place to get away from the daily grind since I heard you were a fan of senior doggies. Honestly, that's just the kind of friend I am, always looking out for everyone else.

Right now it's just me and seventeen other rescue pup friends. Of course, me being the amazing son I am, I opened up my home to my mama too. You see I'm a family man like you – another similarity. Really it's uncanny how much we have in common if you think about it. You sing country music. I live in the country. You eat food. I love cheeseburgers. You have eight million people who follow you, I have twelve thousand people who follow me, which in dog numbers is 84 million (sorry I'm a little more popular than you, but don't be jealous I really like your music too). I mean the list goes on and on.

Anyways back to my invite to The Barn. It's nothing super lavish, just filled with couches, dog beds, a really great open living style environment, filled with the best servants ever who cater to your every need. I'll be honest. They totally spoil me and between you and me I don't even pay them. How about that? They do it all because they love me. Ha! Groupies are the best!

Well, back to me, I'm really like you too because I'm all about giving back when I can. I help take care of my pups and other peeps in The Barn and the pound. Like I said earlier, since I'm kind of a big deal and you're kind of a big deal I thought we should definitely meet up and share a cheeseburger, or two. I mean what better way to bond? Two brothers from another mother sharing a couple burgers together on a farm in a Little Red Barn down in Spring Hill, KS. Wow, that sounds like a hit country song! Feel free to take all the copyrights. #Yourewelcome

Anyways, I won't keep you long. I'm sure you're probably busy, but if you need a break from your celebrity status and want to hang with a pup who really knows how hard it is to be incredibly popular, you're welcome here anytime.

Have your people call my people and they'll hook you up. I even have my own personal driver named Craig who is on call 24/7. How 'bout them apples? I really do have the life — although I'm still waiting for my forever family to find me. But until someone is willing to love me and my mama, Gumpsville will have to do.

Sincerely – your new bff,

Gump aka my celebrity names, Gumpers, Gumperoni, Goo Goo, the Gump Man, Gumpy

PS don't forget to bring the cheeseburgers when you come. See you soon!

#bringLuketothefarm

#adoptasenior

#sharethispost

#doitforGumpy

18-Oct-2019

Hey Luke Bryan — if you need my main man Craig to pick you up just let me know. I've got wheels and all kinds of hook ups.

#BringLuketothefarm

#Gumpyiswaiting

#haveLukespeoplecallGumpspeople

#dontforgetthecheeseburgers

18-Oct-2019

Hey Luke Bryan — Gumpers here. Since you didn't respond to my note about my personal driver picking you up earlier, how about I come and pick you up myself? Don't worry, I've only had a couple DCUIs (devouring cheeseburgers while under the influence). What can I say, I never claimed to be perfect.

Even though my days are pretty busy with napping, sun tanning, eating and looking ridiculously handsome for the camera and fans, I'll make the time for you because I'm a pretty selfless man. Just let me know.

Okay gotta run now. I'm off to visit the seventy other foster rescue pups in Always & Furever care. They really appreciate my celebrity guest appearances to lighten their hearts until their forever families come along. Let's face it, not everyone gets to have their own farm called Gumpsville like me. And I don't even charge an appearance fee (although donations are always encouraged to keep Gumpsville going). The Gump man is by the people and for his people, so I do it out of the kindness of my heart.

Anyways LMK if you want me to swing by when you're in town and I'll pick you up. Gotta put the phone down now. One too many tickets for texting and driving too.

#ithappens

#bringLuketothefarm

#makeGumpysdreamcometrue

#theywillpickupcheeseburgerstogether

#whatsonemoreDCUIforGumpy

19-Oct-2019

Sooooooo Luke. It's me Gump again. I'm headed out for a bit to do a celebrity appearance at some fancy affair and just wanted to drop you a line and remind you about coming to the farm when you're in town.

You see I'm not sure how this happened but I semi-sorta-kinda... what I mean to say is I may have completely accidentally/slightly on purpose promised all of my barn pup pals that you'd stop by. Please don't let them down.

I have no idea how or why they think you're coming but they may have been led to believe that we were already bffs and very well could be soulmates so they are all expecting you to come.

Please don't break their hearts. You can break mine if you want. But not theirs. Please come Luke. Do it for the doggies who aren't as popular as me and need to feel important. Do it for them. Help them help themselves. You can make their dreams come true. They need you. They need me. They need us. Let's do this together.

We'll all be waiting to hear from you. Just imagine Gump and Luke together = Team Guke. That really has a snazzy ring to it. I like it. See you soon.

#TeamGuke

#makeallGumpsfriendsdreamscometrue

#BringLuketothefarm

19-Oct-2019

Luke — buddy bro homie doggeroni, wanna play a game? Sweet...I knew you'd say yes.

True or False:

Always & Furever opened in May 2018. I was the first pup to enter the farm, and am directly responsible for saving 475 dogs lives.

And the answer is........MOSTLY true. It's crazy how A&F opened just seventeen months ago and has saved so many lives! I was actually the fourteenth pup to enter the farm but there is a one in that number and I'm a #1 kind of guy so that is mostly true too. I have personally saved the lives of 475 pups in need, just by being a part of this amazing rescue.

You're gonna wanna know a guy like me. I know people who know people who literally save peoples' lives. Yes Luke. Dogs are people too. Please keep up. They do it simply because these people know me and how much I love other doggies. Quite frankly, I told them to do it. So in my own way, I'm a hero of sorts. I don't want to brag — I'm too humble for that. But if people want to call me a hero, I understand why.

Okay Luke, I gotta go. I think I smell a cheeseburger. #teamGuke #bringLuketothefarm #makeGumpiesdreamscometrue

20-Oct-2019

Hey Luke! My main man Lukie Pookie. Brother from another mother who always shares the peanut butter...Luke the Duke... It's your old buddy Gumpers again. Sorry about the nicknames. I get called so many names by my crazed fans. I think its contagious because sometimes it just slips out. I don't even notice when its happening. I'll never do it again. I promise.

So Luker Pooper, some people might think I'm stalking you and it's okay for common folks to think like that — I get it — but they don't realize it's not considered stalking if someone famous is doing it. So I'm exempt.

And I have to say you're my absolute favorite artist. I've been practicing some of your songs. I especially like that one "when you're a celebrity, it's adios reality, you can act just like a fool and people think you're cool."

Wait... oh crudders.... Mama just told me some guy named Brad sings that and not you. Well shoot. Now this is a bit awkward. For you, not for me. It's still a pretty great song.

No harm no foul right, Lukey Shoopy?

Anyway... my driver offered to chauffeur me to where we think you might be. Even though he's my seven-foot tall super intimidating bodyguard, I promise it's totally legit. Just shoot me your address and we will use this thing called Google Maps to find you. That will save him from putting another 11k miles on his car (from driving all the other pups we've saved on freedom runs and vet trips).

Then once we're together, just like it's meant to be, sharin a cheeseburger with my brother, whose not too manly to cuddle, just chillin in a car, with Gump's bodyguard and the windows open and the sun shining down. Two country celebrity boys turning common folks frowns upside down (well gosh darn it, I did it again, another hit country song just flew out of my mouth) #yourewelcomeagain Someone really needs to write this stuff down. Sometimes I swear I spit out liquid gold.

I'll wait for you to text me your address. If you see Craig and me driving around slowly please don't call the police. It's just your good friend Gumpers trying to spend some quality time with his besty Lukey Bo Poopey.

Team Guke for life! See you soon!

#bringLuketothefarm

#dontletGumpyendupinjailforcelebritystalking

#wewillbailyouout

#hemaybelosingit

#makeGumpsdreamscometrue

#teamGuke

20-Oct-2019

Someday my Luke will come......

#bringLuketothefarm

#apupcandream

#makeGumpysdreamcometrue

#TeamGuke

21-Oct-2019

Top Ten Reasons Why Luke Bryan and Gump should be best friends (according to Gump):

1. FREE LABOR: Gump is willing to help Luke with daily chores (i.e. if Luke's maid quits, Gump will clean up the kitchen floor of any food scraps and is even willing to rid the fridge of any leftovers #selfless)

2. SAFETY: Gump will make Luke feel safer at home. How could he not feel safe with ninety pounds of plumpy Gumpy on his lap or at his feet?

3. PHYSIQUE: Gump will help Luke get in better shape. If Luke would like a more manly physique like the Gumpman, this is what Gump recommends: long naps, big meals, short walks and frequent snacks = the recipe for Gump's frumpy stumpy studly boy-chew-toy sexy bod #alltheladiesloveit

4. FRIENDSHIP: Gump is a true friend. Luke would know Gump is not just using him for his popularity #becauseGumpismorepopular

#accordingtoGump He'd give an arm and a leg, literally, for any of his barn pups (right now he's only had to give one arm #phew). Gump is also an incredible advocate of spray cheese for all doggies. #Heroamongsthispeople

5. APPEARANCES: All the ladies love Gump (yes Gump knows Luke is not a lady but it never hurts to have another handsome man to add to his entourage).

6. SECURITY: Gump would be a great bodyguard on stage (Gump has an amazing sneak attack: a shuffle up to the back of someone's leg signature bite move that is a highly specialized/secret Kung Fu doggie classic move that would literally save Luke's life). If Luke likes being alive Gump highly recommends bringing him everywhere he goes #forLukessake

7. HEALTH: If Luke is sick Gump can make his illness heal faster (i.e. when someone brings Luke chicken soup, Gump is willing to eat all of the chicken so Luke eats only the broth and thus heals faster) #onceagainselfess #GumpwoulddothatforLuke #teamGuke

8. CHEESEBURGERS: According to the old Chinese proverb.... any man who loves cheeseburgers is a man you want in your life. Lucky for Luke, Gump loves cheeseburgers. #Gumpsakeeper.

9. LOYALTY: Gump is loyal. Gump loves everyone, and everyone loves Gump. #Amanamongstallmen

10. THAT SMILE: When Gump smiles, the whole world smiles too. #Truth

Those are the top ten reasons why Luke would definitely want a pup like Gump around.

#TeamGuke

#bffsforlife

#bringLuketothefarm

#dontforgetthecheeseburgers

#andwhowouldntwantafriendwithapolkadottongue

#bonus

22-Oct-2019

My Dearest Luke,

It's been so very long since I've heard your voice.

Yes Luke, I know I can turn on a radio, but we both know it's not the same thing. Where are you, Luke? I write and write, but it's like I'm writing to the wind. My words float off the tip of my tongue into the star-filled skies of the Kansas night and simply vanish.

Oh Luke, there is no use denying it, we were meant to be together. You, me, and my mama. Yes Luke, I know I'm a dog. But if I'm a dog, you're a dog, Luke. If you're a man, I'm a man. We are two star-crossed-souls that have travelled through time. We've defied all odds and dimensions in this journey called life to finally embark upon the chance at a glorious reunion at a Little Red Barn in Spring Hill, KS.

Yes Luke, the fates have kept us apart, but they have also been instrumental in bringing us together. In this moment the whole universe exists solely for that one purpose. You cannot deny the astronomical forces involved. Can you feel that, Luke? It's so very strong. Nothing can separate us, Luke. Because we just know. We are right. We are real. We are meant to be.

Don't fight it, Luke. Go with your Gumpy. When you realize you are meant to spend the rest of your life with someone, you want the rest of your life to start as soon as possible. There is no day like today, Luke, and tomorrow is never guaranteed.

Think about it, Luke. So many life lessons we can teach others together. You make me want to be a better dog. Please respond, Luke. I can only write so many letters. I'm just one dog that lives on a farm and has no hands. So the fact that I'm writing another letter is a miracle in and of itself.

So many things have led to the incredible magic we've created. It's just amazing. I'm amazing, Luke. You're amazing, Luke. Think about how much more amazing we could be together. Gump and Luke. Team Guke Luke.

Just think about it. That's all a dog can ask. I'm just one celebrity, writing to another celebrity, asking him to love him (and his mama) forever. Like Mama always says, life is like a bag of cheeseburgers, you never know what kind of meat you're going to eat.

I'll be waiting for your response, Luke. You had me at cheeseburger. That is all.

Sincerely, your long lost friend,

Gump

PS Luke, the greatest thing you'll ever learn, is just to love Gump and let Gump love you in return. Here's looking at you, Luke.

#teamGukeforlive

#bringLuketothefarm

#helpmakeGumpiesdreamcometrue

23-Oct-2019

Hey Luke Bryan - haven't heard from ya yet buddy, but I've been brainstorming about what I can do for my besty.

I wanted to let you know I'd be willing to open for you at your concert. All I need is some crazy blonde lady driving a riding mower in circles around your audience. I can sing any country tune to pieces. Let me know. I'm ready.

#TeamGuke

#bringGumptotheconcert

#orbringLuketothefarm

#makeGumpiesdreamscometrue

#dontforgetthecheeseburgers

24-Oct-2019

Cue: Theme Music to Mission Impossible

Target: Luke Bryan

Conspirators: Tweedle Dee (alias name Pope Henry III), Tweedle Dum (street name Jaker the Heart Breaker), and of course, the DogFather (human name Gump)

Mission: Bring Luke to the Farm - Execute Team Guke

Motive: To force Luke to be Gump's friend

Location: An undisclosed location containing Little Red Barn filled with slightly delusional talking senior rescue dogs that think they are human.

Fade into Scene:

Dogfather: Ok Tweedles... here's the plan. Tweedle Dee you go out and buy a ginormus bag of cheeseburgers.

Tweedle Dee: You got it boss. What are we going to do with them?

Dogfather: First, and most importantly, once the cheeseburgers arrive, I will eat them.

Tweedle Dee: Hey boss I have no money. How do I buy cheeseburgers?

Dogfather: Don't ask logical questions Tweedle Dee. You know you are not the brains in this barn.

Tweedle Dee: Understood boss, no mulo no problemo. I will look cute and pout and the ladies will shower me with cheeseburgers. Consider it done boss.

Dogfather: Second, and this is most important, we MUST save the bag. Tweedle Dum write that down.

Tweedle Dum: Check. Hey boss I don't know how to write.

Dogfather: Not my problem, just do it. Now, pay attention, October 30th is the day Luke comes to town. This is what's going to go down.... right as Bri is about to leave Tweedle Dee you are going to faint and start twitching uncontrollably — really have to sell it.

Tweedle Dee: Will do boss.

Dogfather: Tweedle Dum, you will start walking in circles until you fall over again and again, get up and repeat. Do not stop until you get the go ahead from me.

Tweedle Dum: You got it.

Dogfather: I will bark one single and solitary time which will cause an astronomical chain reaction beginning with Adam barking which will cause Percy to bark and then within moments the entire barn will be barking. I will then run laps by the window back and forth until I too pass out.

Tweedle Dum: Great plan boss I love it.

Dogfather: I'm not finished. If I was finished this plan would have no purpose.

Tweedle Dum: Good point boss.

Dogfather: Now listen, as a result of the madness Bri will begin to panic. So much so, that she won't leave. Then Jason will come, then they both will call Jane, then Jane will call Nikki, Nikki will call Judy, Judy will call Stephanie, Judy and Stephanie will call Craig while he's on a call with Jane and Nikki, Bri will break out into uncontrollable sobbing from the panic, Jason will run to my aid, and "accidentally" trip over Gumpdrop, hit his head which will result in a 9-1-1 call and the paramedics to arrive and it will be a mad rush to get us to the vet, Jason to the ER, and Bri will need oxygyn to stop the inevitable panic attack. Then, once everyone has arrived it will be frantic and the second they open that second gate Tweedle Dee, you instantly feel better and make a break for it.

Tweedle Dee: Got it boss.

Dogfather: Tweedle Dum, same thing but make sure to keep selling it until Craig goes to pick you up and then as he nears you steal Craig's keys. You have to be sneaky subtle.

Tweedle Dum: Great plan Bossman because I definitely don't want to go to the vet.

Dogfather: No one is going to the vet Tweedle Dee. You're faking being sick. You aren't really sick.

Tweedle Dum: Ok phew! Glad of that, Bossman.

Dogfather: (Dogfather shaking his head in frustration, lets out a deep sigh) Back to the plan. Now once they arrive we all get into Craig's limo. This is the second most important part.... Tweedle Dum remember that bag?

Tweedele Dum: What bag?

Dogfather: The bag of cheeseburgers you are going to buy?

Tweedle Dum: Yes boss, the bag with the cheeseburgers you probably won't share with us?

Dogfather: Yes, that bag. Tweedle Dum, you are going to have to swallow the bag on the 29th so that once we are in the car, I will need you to poop it out. Preferably not in pieces.

Tweedle Dee: Oh sheesh boss, I just don't know about that, I've never been able to poop on demand before.

Dogfather : Yes you have. Jason has the video of it. Now back to the plan.......we will then head to Luke's concert.

Tweedle Dee: Whoop whoop! Fantastic plan boss I love his music.

Dogfather: No Tweedle Dee, we aren't going to listen to his music. We're headed to the concert to kidnap Luke and we'll use that bag to throw over his head when we hold him hostage......

Tweedle Dee and Tweedle Dum: Genius boss. Brilliant. No better plan on earth.

What will happen next? Will the Dogfather and the Tweedles successfully kidnap Luke Bryan? Will Jason survive after his horrific fall? Does Bri ever stop panicking? Does Craig even realize the Dogfather stole his car? So many questions unanswered..... to find out more come back tomorrow.

#bringLuketothefarm

#teamGuke

#makeGumpiesdreamcometrue

Note: This FB post/conversation contains hypothetical/fantasy situations and to our knowledge by no means, way shape or form does anyone (human or animal) at the undisclosed location containing a Little Red Barn actually intend to kidnap Luke Bryan.

This message will self-destruct in T-Minus 24 hours.

24-Oct-2019

Luke Bryan — a response to one of my notes would be nice. Just sayin. The Gump Man has feelings too. Sheesh.

I'm just going to sulk until you respond. I never said I was above pouting. If someone wants to rub my belly while I wait, I'd be okay with that.

That is all.

#helpGumpturnthatfrownupsidedown

#rubhisbelly

#makeGumpiesdreamcometrue

#bringLuketothefarm

25-Oct-2019

Hey there my ole buddy Luke Bryan — how about we play fun fact about the Little Red Barn?

The farm was originally named "Gumpland" after me but now it's also commonly referred to as Gumpsville.

Some people like to call it the Ever After Farm because they believe it's never too late for happily ever after. They believe all dogs deserve a home and no old dog should die in a shelter. Yada... yada... yada....

You and I both know the truth. People can think what they want.

And that's today's Fun Fact With Gumpers.

#bringLuketothefarm

#hemaybelosingitwithouthim

#itsallaboutGumpy

#makeGumpsdreamscometrue

28-Oct-2019

Four scientifically proven facts about Gump that would make Luke Bryan become his best friend instantaneously if he ever were so lucky enough to meet him....

1) GUMP SMELLS GOOD. No one wants a stinky friend hanging around them. Hygiene and cleanliness are very important to Gump, AND he uses spray cheese to floss daily. #Notmeannotleanbuta-cleanmachine

2) GUMP IS GENUINE. Gump isn't materialistic. He doesn't waste money on clothes, cars, or flashy items to show his fame. He keeps it real. He only puts money toward spray cheese, peanut butter and cheeseburgers. #Thenecessities

3) GUMP IS AUTHENTIC. What you see is what you get. He lets it all hang out and never listens to the fat shamers on social media. He is comfortable with who he is and loves himself for how God made him. #Whodoesntloveadogwiththreelegs

4) GUMP IS EASY GOING. Gump clearly has a fantastic sense of humor, can roll with the punches, and believes in not taking life too seriously. He enjoys smelling and peeing on the roses, long walks down the driveway and short naps before heading back. He loves a good belly laugh after stealing a piece of pizza, and never ever EVER says no to an extra piece of cake. #Letallthedogseatcake

And those are the four scientifically proven facts why Gump is the man to know.

#gottatrustaguywithapolkadottongue

#BringLuketothefarm

#makeGumpiesdreamcometrue

While our attempts to lure the country singer to The Barn were unsuccessful, we did increase our exposure and expand our audience. For that, we are grateful.

We even added a new foster in his honor.

LUKE BRYAN (LB)

LUKE BRYAN's Story

(As by The Daniels, his foster family)

Luke Bryan came to The Barn in the fall of 2019 after being rescued from a high kill shelter in Wichita. His arrival (and new name) coincided with the country music singer's Farm Tour concert scheduled later that month.

Although Luke is allergic to cats, he gets along well with other dogs and is loving toward people of all ages. He gets allergy shots and takes them like a champ.

Luke is a wonderful guard dog who only barks at strangers. And like his namesake, Luke loves to sing along with passing sirens, howling until they are out of earshot.

Luke's passions include snoring, sleeping, and being a couch potato. His furever family is certainly out there and will be blessed to have him in their home.

Everyone thinks they
have the best dog, and
none of them are wrong.

~ W R Purche

And in keeping with the humorous theme of this man/dog celebrity duo, the Daniels' also posted this mock interview:

Luke Bryan 👨 and Luke Bryan 🐕 were recently interviewed together on the radio station PAWS. I thought I'd share the transcript with you:

Good morning and a special welcome to our guests today—Luke Bryan 👨 and Luke Bryan 🐕.

How are you both doing this morning?

LB 👨: Good, good.

LB 🐕: Life's not ruff.

Great, well, are you ready for some fan questions?

LB 👨: Sure!

LB 🐕: (tail wags and ears perk up)

Could you tell our listeners what you do?

LB 😀: Well, I'm known as a country singer and songwriter.

LB 🐕: I'm a dog. I do dog stuff.

And how old are you?

LB 😀: 43

LB 🐕: I hear I'm 5 or 6, but I don't really know. Age is just a number, right?

Tell us about your family.

LB 😀: Of course! My wife Caroline and I are going on 14 years together with 2 sons.

LB 🐕: I'm single and ready to mingle, but no puppies are in my future. Someone took that option off the table.

What's your net worth?

LB 😀: Well, that's kind of personal, isn't it?

LB 🐕: I'm PRICELESS!

What are some of your hobbies?

LB 😀: Hunting, fishing, watching movies, you know, the usual.

LB 🐕: Well, basically sleep, snore, and snuggle. Occasionally I like to bark at things through the fence, but barking inside isn't really my thing.

Any tattoos?

LB 😀: Yeah, I have a few.

LB 🐕: No, but I do have a cool heart on my neck.

Can you describe your stomach?

LB 😀: That seems like a weird question...

LB 🐈: My stomach is super soft and I love to get it rubbed. Want to rub it for me?

Any bathroom habits we should know about?

LB 👤: Um...no?

LB 🐈: I do all my business outside. No inside accidents for me!

What are you looking for in life?

LB 👤: Love, happiness, health...

LB 🐈: A family to love me. I love kids, adults, and dogs. Cats aren't my thing. I have some allergies so I need a home that'll help me manage those with my food and my meds. I'm a big love bug who just wants to snuggle and spend my life with a family who will love me.

Well, you heard it here folks! Thanks for listening in today!

DISCLAIMER: Luke Bryan's 👤 information was verified online or made up for comedic purposes. Luke Bryan's 🐈 information was directly quoted from him. Luke Bryan 👤 declined a photo opportunity, but Luke Bryan 🐈 had no problem sharing his selfies!

PART SIX
HOW YOU CAN HELP

Dogs just need love. That's all.
~ Jennifer Westfield

A FEW SUGGESTIONS...

To FULFILL ITS MISSION, The Barn depends on the generosity of others. No donation is too small. No skill too mundane. No service hours too few. The Barn is grateful for any help. Give what you can and watch God multiply the efforts.

Here are a few ways you can help:

- **Pray** for the dogs, the volunteers, the medical teams, our financial resources.
- **Like our Facebook page**: facebook.com/nevertoolateforhappilyeverafter
- **Like our Facebook posts**
- **Love our Facebook posts** (Facebook algorithms give more visibility to hearts than the default thumbs-up)
- **Share our posts** on your timeline to increase visibility
- **Donate money** (alwaysandfurever.love/donate)
- **Give a one-time donation** — the cost of a cup of coffee (alwaysandfurever.love/donate)

- **Give an ongoing monthly donation** (alwaysandfurever.love/donate)
- **Sponsor a boarding dog**
- **Donate supplies** by using our Amazon wishlist. You can request shipment directly to The Barn (23595 W 223rd St – Spring Hill, KS – 66083)
- **Volunteer at The Barn**
- First attend one of the mandatory volunteer training sessions. Then you are free to come out and love on the dogs anytime (and help with a few ongoing chores such as laundry and poop patrol)
- Don't forget to share the dogs' photos on social media
- Take a dog on a special outing to the park for a walk and/or Sonic for a cheeseburger and pup cup treat
- **Other Volunteer Services**
- Freedom Drivers help transport rescued dogs from their current location to The Barn.
- Vet Drivers help transport dogs from The Barn or boarding to vet appointments
- Construction/Handyman/Lawn Care services on an as-needed basis
- Any other special talent/service/interest you may wish to volunteer. Contact info@alwaysandfurever.love to let us know.
- **Foster a dog** until we can find a furever home. Complete the online form (alwaysandfurever.love/forms). Fostering a dog makes room at The Barn to rescue one more.
- If you can't foster indefinitely, consider a weekend foster opportunity to allow the dogs a break from The Barn.
- **Adopt a dog**. Complete an online form (alwaysandfurever.love/forms). Adopting one dog saves two lives.

THANK YOU

Faith built this Little Red Barn. Through the darkest times we know light will always shine again.

I learned years ago that life without hope isn't a life at all. This belief extends to our precious animals. If all we ever do is give them hope of a better future filled with love, then absolutely everything is worth it.

Dreams can come true. If you are willing to put in the work and lead with love, you will never be a failure. It is truly never too late for happily ever after. You may need to adapt. You may need to reimagine the dream. But all things are possible for those who keep the faith and never give up.

I wish I could personally thank everyone who made this Little Red Barn the magical place it is today. But there are too many people on earth and in heaven that have made this dream possible. So let me simply say, to all those who support our pups and cats, thank you. You are truly appreciated.

~ Jen Dulski

Made in the USA
Monee, IL
09 October 2021